COUNTERPOINT

Books by Walter Piston

HARMONY

COUNTERPOINT

ORCHESTRATION

COUNTERPOINT

BY *Walter Piston*

W · W · NORTON & COMPANY

New York · London

Musical Illustrations drawn by
MARIO CARMOSINO

W. W. Norton & Company, Inc., 500 Fifth Avenue, New York, N.Y. 10110
W. W. Norton & Company Ltd., 37 Great Russell Street, London WC1B 3NU

ISBN 0 393 09728 5

PRINTED IN THE UNITED STATES OF AMERICA
FOR THE PUBLISHERS BY THE VAIL-BALLOU PRESS
4 5 6 7 8 9 0

TO
A. TILLMAN MERRITT

CONTENTS

INTRODUCTION 9

1. THE MELODIC CURVE 13

2. MELODIC RHYTHM 26

3. THE HARMONIC BASIS 40

4. HARMONIC RHYTHM 60

5. TWO-PART COUNTERPOINT 72

6. MOTIVE STRUCTURE 99

7. THREE-PART COUNTERPOINT 118

8. COUNTERPOINT IN MORE THAN THREE PARTS 143

9. INVERTIBLE COUNTERPOINT 167

10. CANON IN TWO PARTS 188

11. OTHER TYPES OF CANON 208

CONCLUSION 228

INDEX 233

INTRODUCTION

THE art of counterpoint is the art of combining melodic lines. The contrapuntal essence, as an ingredient of inner vitality in music is, however, something deeper than a process of manipulation and combination, and it is to be found in nearly all music. That is to say, most music is to some degree contrapuntal.

Implicit in the term contrapuntal, by origin, is the idea of disagreement. The interplay of agreement and disagreement between the various factors of the musical texture constitutes the contrapuntal element in music. The study of counterpoint involves a study of these qualities of agreement and disagreement, or, to put it differently, of dependence and independence.

For example, dependence, or agreement, would be supplied harmonically by the use of consonances and by coincidence of harmonic rhythm with melodic rhythm. In rhythm, there would be coincidence of stresses or strong beats, and of rhythmic activity. In the melodic lines, there would be what is called similar motion, and the climax, or peak, would be reached simultaneously by different voices. These features detract from the contrapuntal nature of the texture.

On the other hand, independence, or disagreement, is obtained by the use of dissonances and non-harmonic tones; by avoiding coincidence of rhythmic stress and rhythmic patterns; by opposition of the melodic curves, making use of oblique and contrary motion. These are some of the means contributing to the contrapuntal style.

Contrapuntal procedure differs according to the composer's attitude toward these rather complex elements of dependence and independence. A common practice in counterpoint such as that found in the harmony of the eighteenth and nineteenth centuries does not exist. Throughout that period, differences in the chords used, and in the

9

manner of their use, are not significant enough to invalidate the description of a harmonic practice common to all composers of the period, whereas the treatment of contrapuntal elements by these same composers shows the widest possible divergence.

Historically, there are three outstanding peaks in the art of counterpoint. The first was the virtually "absolute" polyphony of the Gothic period, and the elaborate and virtuoso counterpoint of the Franco-Flemish schools that followed. The second was the music of the latter half of the sixteenth century as exemplified by Palestrina, while the third, that of the Baroque, is summed up in the works of Johann Sebastian Bach.

The first of the periods mentioned has ceased to exert an active influence on our music, but Palestrina and Bach have become the very symbols of polyphony. A moment's consideration of the work of these two men reveals the existence of two distinct types of approach, two distinct contrapuntal attitudes, or contrapuntal styles. Both of these styles are of supreme importance in the development of the art of music and the study of both kinds of contrapuntal writing is indispensable to all musicians and students of music. It will be the purpose of the present study, however, to examine only that type of contrapuntal technique which is so well represented by J. S. Bach.

"Sixteenth century counterpoint," more properly the counterpoint of the so-called Palestrina style, has been excellently treated in published studies by such scholars as Jeppesen, Merritt, and Morris, so that further general contributions to the subject at this time would be superfluous. The Palestrina style is a specific vocal polyphony within well-defined limits and restrictions. The presence of a text means the introduction of an extra-musical element, and one which furnishes the rhythmic basis for the music to a large extent. The preoccupation with harmonic materials, too, is greatly restricted compared to the idiom practiced in the last centuries. We should not, therefore, expect this music to show us the principles applied in the great bulk of musical literature much nearer to our time.

While the study of the Palestrina style of contrapuntal writing is of inestimable value, not only to the choral composer, but to all students of music, there are many reasons why a study of the kind of counterpoint seen at its best in the music of Bach is needed. This harmonic, rhythmic, instrumental attitude toward the contrapuntal texture is not only typical of Bach's immediate predecessors, but one may safely assert that most composers after Bach, including those of the present century, have looked up to his manner as the ideal of contrapuntal technique. We must not forget that the essential purpose of technical studies in music is to discover how music has been written, rather than to say how it should be written in the future. Here, then, is the literature of some three hundred years to form the logical basis for a study of counterpoint.

Traditional treatises and courses in counterpoint pay slight attention to harmony and rhythm, and do not, as a rule, turn to actual compositions for examples and principles. The styles adopted vary from an archaic, modal style to that of a speculative modernity. In general there is inadequate preparation for the study of the fugue, so that students find themselves at a loss in trying to reconcile the procedures of Bach with what they have learned of counterpoint. But the fundamental shortcoming in practically all the traditional methods is that they do not seek to impart knowledge of the practice of composers, but to put forth directions for the writing of music, despite the truth that no person can know how music will be written even ten years hence.

It may be helpful to add a word of warning that this is not to be a study of Bach's personal style. The inclusive character of his creative output as well as its effective excellence makes it inevitable that more examples will be drawn from his works than from those of any other composer. But the effort should continually be made to include as many composers as possible in the investigation of the various principles involved in contrapuntal writing.

Even though we cannot say that there is a common practice in counterpoint among the composers of the last three hundred years, the differences are not in the elements and principles but in the degree of their application. It is hoped that the study of these elements and principles will be helpful to an understanding of music of all times, especially new contemporary music, and that composers may be stimulated thereby to contribute their own individual practice in the matter of contrapuntal procedure.

The student is cautioned not to make a fetish of counterpoint or to look upon the term contrapuntal as synonymous with good. Much of the world's great music is but slightly contrapuntal. Furthermore, the contrapuntal quality itself is not absolute, and it varies greatly even in works distinctly recognized as contrapuntal, such as a Bach fugue.

As preparation for the study of counterpoint as set forth in this book, it is assumed that the student is well grounded in the principles of harmony. A year's study of harmony should suffice. Knowledge of chromatic chords and of their use is advantageous but not necessary. Most important are the fundamental principles of tonal functions and voice leading. Harmonic formulae and sequences will prove of valuable assistance in the organization of phrases.

The exercises given at the end of each chapter may not be numerous enough to provide adequate practice for some individual needs. They are designed as specimens to show the kind and scope of exercise material to be used. It is expected that further exercises will be devised by the teacher or by the student himself.

Students who have not acquired facility in reading the C clefs (soprano, alto, and tenor) are advised to remedy this deficiency in fundamental musicianship by practice, and to use these clefs in writing exercises in counterpoint. The clefs should be learned if only to be able to read the published works of the great composers, but they are a necessity in score reading and a valuable aid in transposition.

⇥» «⇤

THE MELODIC CURVE

BEFORE proceeding to the combination of two or more melodic lines it is necessary to look into the nature of the melodic line itself. For this purpose let us maintain as far as possible an objective point of view, examining the more technical and tangible characteristics of melody, and leaving for more specialized and philosophical consideration those elusive but nevertheless important values such as emotion, tension, and relaxation. This is not to belittle the force of aesthetic qualities but it is the author's experience and belief that one is best awakened to their presence by ample first-hand contact with music as sound, through playing, singing, and listening. At any rate, it is understood that no attempt will be made here to formulate principles governing subjective attributes of melody.

The outline of a melody may be perceived by simply looking at the music. We permit ourselves the use of the term "melodic curve" to describe this outline, although an accurate graphic representation of a melody would show a series of angular movements. For instance, a scale line ascending in moderate tempo would be pictured as a flight of steps, whereas the musical effect is that of a continuous line in one direction. So the word curve is useful to suggest the essential quality of continuity, and to emphasize that minor decorations and indentations do not affect the main course of the melodic line.

The amount of melodic line taken as a unit for analysis, as well as for written exercises, coincides in general with the length of a phrase, which allows for a great deal of variation. The question of what constitutes a melodic unit will be answered through discussion of its several features and by means of examples.

By far the most usual type of melodic curve is that seen in the example below by Beethoven.

EX. 1. Beethoven—*String Quartet, op. 18, no. 1*

This curve rises from its lowest tone A to the high point B-flat, reached in the fifth measure, and it comes to rest on the C-sharp, a note in the lower half of its range of a ninth. The curve is a "wavy" curve, having the lesser high points F and G, as it ascends, and again F in the seventh measure. These lesser high points are given added prominence rhythmically and their relationship in pitch to one another is an important feature of the melodic outline.

It is to be remarked that most of the melodic movement is stepwise, there being but five intervals larger than a second in the entire phrase. These are three minor thirds, one perfect fourth, and one diminished seventh. As more melodies are studied, one observes that the rule is stepwise motion, skips being used for variety.

Following are two more examples of this type of melodic curve. They differ from the melody by Beethoven in the location of the high point in the curve. In the first of the two examples the highest part of the line is somewhat nearer to the beginning, the descent being more gradual, whereas in the second case the peak of the curve is found just at the half-way point in the phrase.

EX. 2. J. S. Bach—*Well-tempered Clavier, I, Fugue no. 13*

EX. 3. Johann Christian Bach—*Sinfonia, op. 18, no. 4*

The melodic curve shown below is of a much less common type.

EX. 4. J. S. Bach—*Concerto for Two Violins*

This is the reverse of the Beethoven example, beginning and ending high, the curve bending down to its lowest point near the middle of the melody.

EX. 5. Mozart—*Rondo, K. 511*

The curve of this melody by Mozart may be said to combine the principles of the two types first described. Its first part resembles the curve of example no. 4, but its high point comes in the next to last measure, followed by a rather rapid descent.

EX. 6. Chopin—*Impromptu, op. 51*

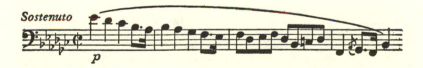

Some melodic phrases start with the high point and end low, as in the above. Examples of this precedure are not relatively numerous, however.

EX. 7. Mendelssohn—*String Quartet, op. 80*

This excerpt shows a phrase starting at the low point and ending at the highest. With this type of ascending line, a crescendo is generally expected, following the natural tendency of all forms of speech to combine increasing loudness with rising pitch. Indeed, this natural rule is noticeable in the application of dynamics to most music. Anyone who has had experience in conducting instrumental groups knows what constant attention is necessary to prevent even fine players from playing louder when the music rises in pitch. This is not the place for extended discussion of the matter of dynamic indications, but students should make note of the effect produced whenever a composer asks for a nuance contrary to this natural tendency.

Example no. 8 has also this kind of line, rising gradually to end on the high point. The beginning is a little different since the first motive touches the middle of the range. As we know, Bach gave no dynamic indications for this music.

EX. 8. J. S. Bach—*Well-tempered Clavier, I, Fugue no. 16*

RANGE

Melodic lines having a narrow pitch range give a somewhat level impression when compared with the wider curves in the above examples. As a general rule there will, however, be high and low points to give shape to the outline. Note in the following example by Bach the relationship between the high points B-flat and C in the first two measures and their eventual destination C-sharp, D, in the fourth measure. The relationship between the low points D, C, D, C-sharp, D, is in this instance more static in effect. This continuity through the low points will be noticed by the ear but is always less important than the high point relationships.

EX. 9. J. S. Bach—*B-Minor Mass, Agnus Dei*

PITCH LOCATION

The range in pitch of the melodic line is naturally determined by the medium for which it is written, so that no rule can be given beyond the observation that extreme notes of the instrumental range are sparingly used. Rather more essential than the mechanical limitation of range is the question of tessitura, or pitch location. A melodic line will ordinarily possess a feeling of balance about some general level of pitch. It is not necessary or practicable to try to determine this point exactly. In a general way, we may assume that the pitch location of a melody is to be found halfway between its highest and lowest tones, although several quantitative and qualitative factors would have to be taken into consideration if a more precise definition of the point of balance were sought.

Lines with wide range run the risk of becoming unstable in this matter of pitch balance. A change of pitch location is to be expected if different parts of the range of an instrument are to be utilized, but this usually means a change of phrase as well. The melodic unit, or phrase, is as a rule balanced on a single pitch location.

In the following example there is no doubt that the pitch balance swings around a point in the vicinity of the fourth space of the staff, despite the wide range of two octaves and a half. Oscillation between the extremes of the range is one way to make certain of a clear balance.

EX. 10. Schumann—*The Prophet Bird, op. 82*

The balance of the phrase below, by Haydn, with a range of about the same extent, is less clear. The first four measures establish a pitch location which will not do for the last two measures. The introduction of a new pitch location causes a break in the unity of the phrase, in this case no doubt desired by the composer, since there is a varied repetition of that part of the phrase beginning with the group of sixteenth-notes in the second measure.

EX. 11. Haydn—*String Quartet, op. 2, no. 5*

Not all instrumental melodies have a wide range. Possibilities in the construction of a melodic curve within the range of a major sixth are shown in this example by Brahms. Melodic interest and variety are achieved through subtle rhythmic treatment of six tones.

EX. 12. Brahms—*Symphony no. 3*

MELODIC SKIPS

Melodic intervals of all kinds and sizes are found in instrumental writing, even an occasional skip of more than an octave. In example no. 10 may be seen such unusual intervals as the diminished tenth, diminished fourth, and augmented third. Such chromatic intervals will be the result of the harmonic style adopted or, as in this case, will be created by the introduction of chromatic non-harmonic tones.

Wide skips tend to break the continuity of the line, and are elements of variety in the curve. After an interval as large as a seventh or octave, the line nearly always turns back in the direction opposite to that of the skip, thus helping to keep the pitch balance within the range of the large skip. In the following melody the pitch balance, as well as the graceful quality of the curve, seem unusually satisfactory.

EX. 13. Mozart.—*String Quartet, K. 428*

EX. 14. Corelli—*Sonata a Tre, op. 3, no. 1*

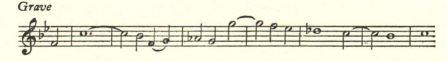

In the Corelli example the upward octave skip is both preceded and followed by downward stepwise movement. Note the similar balancing and unifying effect of the third note of the melody, turning inward after the skip of a fifth, and likewise the upward turn after the downward skip of a fourth in measure three.

Another example by Mozart shows this principle of change of direction after a large skip, this time the skip of a tenth.

EX. 15. Mozart—*String Quartet, K. 421*

Exceptions to this rule can of course be found. This quotation from Bruckner's Fourth Symphony does not conform. Note the fine melodic curve and the important relationship between the high points C-sharp and D.

EX. 16. Bruckner—*Symphony no. 4*

The following is an example of a momentary break in the line, caused by the apparent change in pitch location in the eighth measure. The threatened break is saved by the reappearance of A-flat in the next to last measure. A real break would result if D were played instead of this A-flat, which acts as a continuation of the A-flat sounded two bars before.

EX. 17. Haydn—*String Quartet, op. 9, no. 2*

SMALLER MELODIC UNITS

A common type of line is that in which the melodic unit seems to be broken up into several smaller units, each giving its own cadential impression. In the phrase below, the line comes to a stop in the middle of the first full measure and again in the second. Obviously such a melody does not possess the degree of continuity found in example no. 1, for instance. Relationships are nevertheless heard between high and low points throughout the phrase.

EX. 18. Schubert—*Symphony no. 5*

Similarly the following melodic line, although very naturally divisible into two balancing and complementary melodic units, exhibits a well-organized coherence and form, both in the curve of the melody and in the correspondences between prominent points.

EX. 19. Mozart.—*Piano Concerto, K. 459*

Prominent points in the melody will often form in the mind of the listener a simplified or fundamental melodic thread, other tones being heard as decorations of this elementary line. Example no. 21 traces just such a fundamental succession of the important tones found in the melody of example no. 20.

EX. 20. Handel—*Firework Music, Overture*

EX. 21

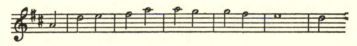

It is interesting and instructive to experiment by applying other decorative tones to the line as given in example 21, and to derive similar fundamental melodic designs from melodies given in other examples. The student should be warned, however, against overemphasis on this aspect of melodic analysis. The individual and definitive form of the melody as left by the composer is all-important. It may be of interest to find that two different melodies can be reduced to the same simple scale line, but the value of this as a discovery can be, and often is, greatly overestimated. Furthermore, it is notorious that no expressive medium can compare to music for adaptability to predetermined analytical patterns. In music almost any formula sought can be found and made to fit. It is well to be watchful lest we be deceived by this flexibility. It is important to see that in the process of analysis and simplification we do not destroy or lose sight of those details of a melody which are the essence of its individuality and expressive quality.

COMPOUND CURVE

If the principle of relationships between high points (and between low points) is further developed, a type of melodic construction is arrived at in which we sense two lines in what appears on paper to be but one. This may be called a compound melodic line. It is used most often by Bach and it adds greatly to the richness of his contrapuntal texture.

EX. 22. J. S. Bach—*Concerto for Two Violins*

The relationships recognized by the ear in this compound line might be represented by the following version in two-part counterpoint.

EX. 23

STUDENTS' WORK

Exercises are intended primarily for the clarification, through experience, of the principles under discussion. One must, therefore, be prepared to reject as irrelevant even the most inspired and beautiful musical offering unless it answers the question asked. Likewise, one should not expect too much over and above what is asked. Especially in the earlier chapters of this book, broad allowance should be made for differences in musical background and technical attainments on the part of students.

The points raised in this chapter have to do only with the melodic outline and they can be applied in a variety of harmonic and rhythmic styles. The examples are meant to suggest the general limits of the style of the music upon which we are to base our observations of contrapuntal practice. Students are advised that to attempt exercises in a style of writing which departs radically from what he sees in the examples given in this book will, while it may prove diverting for the moment, seriously reduce the effectiveness of this as a study of counterpoint.

All exercises must be written for some known medium. Employ any instruments with whose range and sound you are at least moderately familiar. Details of special instrumental technique and tone color are beside the point here.

All exercises must be given tempo indications as well as dynamic markings. In short, each exercise is to be thought of as real music, moving at a given pace, sounding at a given degree of loudness or softness, and being played on a designated instrument.

The natural tendency of beginners in writing melodies is to be "short winded." One may therefore suggest that it is better to err on the side of greater length of line, trying to achieve the longest line that will not break. Remember that stepwise movement is for unity and skips for variety. Avoid too many repeated notes, or too much prominence given to any one note.

EXERCISES

1. Construct three different phrases having the general type of curve shown in example no. 1.

2. Construct melodic lines exemplifying the types of curve shown in the examples nos. 4, 6, and 7.

3. Construct a melodic phrase having a range not exceeding a minor sixth.

4. Construct a melodic phrase employing at least one skip of an octave.

5. Construct a melodic phrase having a range of two octaves and a third, with a pitch location balanced on a point approximately an octave above middle C.

CHAPTER TWO

MELODIC RHYTHM

THE important subject of rhythm in music has not as yet been clearly and adequately treated in any published work known to the present writer. The existing literature by its contradictions and complexities tends to confusion, engendering misconceptions and fallacies which are all too often perpetuated by teachers of music.

Rhythm being of the essence in counterpoint, a complete study of it would be entirely appropriate here, but unfortunately the limits of space and scope imposed by practical considerations make it impossible to include detailed and exhaustive discussion of this special subject. Description of the fundamental factors of rhythm is offered, entirely without pretense of satisfying the need implied in the preceding paragraph, as a possible basis for continued investigation by the student.

Rhythm in music gives an impression of life and forward movement through the association of strong impulses, accents, beats, or stresses, with weaker ones. These impulses are given out melodically, by the individual parts or voices, and harmonically, by the aggregate effect of the voices sounding together. Rhythmic impulses may also be imparted by percussion, in which case the pattern played by a percussion instrument may be regarded as a melodic rhythm, on a single tone.

METER

In itself, meter has no rhythm. It is simply a means of measuring music, principally for purposes of keeping time, and as an aid in playing or singing together in ensemble music. In placing bar-lines to apply our units of measurement to the music, we select, as far as we can, points where the music seems to have the feeling of an initial pulse. That we find this fairly easy to do, with units of two and three beats, is due to the fact that a large amount of music is regular in pulse, and so we are deceived into assuming that the meter itself is rhythmic, and rules are formulated, some of which are even harmful to the development of rhythmic perception.

As an illustration, beginners are commonly schooled in the principle that, in a measure of four beats, the first beat has the strongest accent, the third beat the next in strength, and the second and fourth the weakest of all. Now this is true only in a very limited number of cases and it is plain to see that the adoption of such a principle would be fatal to a proper execution of this phrase by Chopin:

EX. 24. Chopin—*Nocturne, op. 37, no. 1*

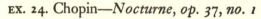

Whatever rhythmic effect is felt here is imparted by the harmonic changes (harmonic rhythm), and there should be no attempt on the part of the performer to let the hearer know where the bar-lines are placed.

The following is an example of melodic rhythm in complete agreement with the meter. That is to say, the strong impulses felt by the listener on each half-note, as compared with the much weaker impulses of the quarter-notes, come at the points where the bar-lines have been placed, marking off the music into metric units equal in time value to three quarter-notes each.

EX. 25. J. S. Bach—*Passacaglia for Organ*

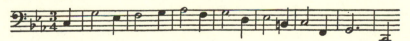

The same sort of agreement between the strong impulses of the melodic rhythm and the location of the bar-lines is present in the next illustration, although it is less obvious to the eye because of the varied time values used in the melody. The strongest impulse does, however, occur consistently on the first beat of each measure.

EX. 26. Haydn—*String Quartet, op. 1, no. 1*

Evidently this cannot be said of the following excerpt, in which some of the measures have no impulse at all on the first beat, notably where a note of the preceding measure has been held over the bar-line.

EX. 27. Schumann—*Symphony no. 3*

In example 28 a much greater degree of melodic freedom can be observed.

Here there is virtually no agreement between the points of rhythmic stress in the melody and the placing of the bar-lines. It is safe to say that if this melody were heard without its accompanying voices one could only guess what metric division the composer had employed in his notation.

EX. 28. J. S. Bach—*French Suite no. 2, Sarabande*

When the melodic rhythm is not in agreement with the meter, the disagreement is more often than not made apparent to the hearer by means of an accompaniment or well established regular pulse, to which the metric divisions stand in closer relationship.

EX. 29. Beethoven—*Symphony no. 8*

Notice that in the first six measures of the above the only first beat struck by the melody is the C in bar four. It is a tone of weaker rhythmic stress than the long F which follows it. This F, by virtue of its length and position in the phrase, and being introduced by skip, is the strongest tone of the melody. Its entrance is not marked by a bar-line, and if it were, a measure different from the three-four measure, indicated by the three recurring accented F's in the preceding bars, would be called for. The accompaniment and established pulse of the movement prevent this melody being heard in this form:

EX. 30

The way in which the melody is introduced over the accompaniment is shown below. Octave doublings in the score have been omitted in this sketch.

EX. 31

STRONG AND WEAK BEATS

The universal custom of beating time to music gives us the terms up-beat, down-beat, strong beat, weak beat. The term down-beat for the initial pulse of a measure of music, provided the bar-line has been prop-erly placed, seems satisfactorily descriptive of the feeling of this initial pulse. It may be likened to the downward motion of a conductor's baton, of a violinist's bow arm, or to the physical action of putting a pencil down on a desk.

In making these motions, however, it is quite possible that the up-beat may be stronger than the down-beat. We may pick up the pencil with a certain force and speed and put it down gently, as well as pick it up gently and set it down heavily. Thus we could illustrate the strong up-beat and the strong down-beat.

The difference need not be violent or exaggerated to be significant. The following shows strong up-beats with weak down-beats. The stress falls upon the second beat of each measure, and the effect here is that of a rhythm of two beats, the second being twice as long as the first.

EX. 32. Brahms—*Sonata for Violin and Piano, op. 100*

In the next example the down-beats are alternately weak and strong, or, to put it another way, the strong beats are alternately up and down.

EX. 33. Schubert—*Symphony no. 4*

When tones of unequal time values are associated, the longer tones usually seem to possess more rhythmic weight than the shorter ones, whether or not they are given more stress by the performer. Thus in example 34 the dotted quarter notes make strong beats by comparison with the eighths.

EX. 34. Beethoven—*Symphony no. 3*

A tone approached through a wide melodic skip will ordinarily give the impression of rhythmic weight, as do the two high B-flats in the following example, and the A-flat in the melody by Schumann.

EX. 35. Mozart—*Sonata, K. 279*

EX. 36. Schumann—*Piano Concerto, op. 54*

Another means of marking a strong beat is the appoggiatura. This is a melodic tone of rhythmic weight which resolves by step into a weaker tone. The resolution takes place most often in a downward direction but chromatically raised or leading-tone type appoggiature resolve upward.

EX. 37. Berlioz—*Fantastic Symphony*

EX. 38. Schubert—*Sonatina for Violin and Piano, op. 137, no. 2*

The appoggiature shown above are of longer time value than their respective notes of resolution. This is not necessarily true of the appoggiatura as some are equal to and even shorter than the note of resolution, but the "leaning" characteristic of strong-to-weak rhythm is always present, as the name suggests.

EX. 39. J. S. Bach—*Well-tempered Clavier, I, Fugue no. 24*

EX. 40. Mozart—*String Quartet, K. 465*

The appoggiatura will be considered in chapter three, especially in its relation to the harmonic background.

Strong accents are sometimes indicated by the composer for special effect, at points which would normally remain unaccented. These are artificial accents, purposely contrary to the natural accentuation of the music. The device was a favorite one with Beethoven and Mozart.

EX. 41. Beethoven—*Sonata, op. 14, no. 2*

EX. 42. Mozart—*String Quartet, K. 387*

THE ANACRUSIS

The group of tones preceding and introducing a down-beat is called anacrusis, or up-beat. The anacrusis may consist of but one or two notes, or it may be quite extensive. In what is perhaps its commonest form it is shorter in time than the note or group of notes forming the down-beat.

EX. 43. Brahms—*Ballade, op. 118, no. 3*

Allegro energico

The rhythmic feeling of anacrusis is not limited to the first up-beat in the phrase. In the following illustration the first group of eighth-notes forms an anacrusis to the A, and the next five eighth-notes constitute an anacrusis to the E. The E is an appoggiatura and hence is a well defined down-beat. We may, therefore, entertain the conception that all of the preceding tones of the phrase have the group function of anacrusis to the E.

EX. 44. Mendelssohn—*Song Without Words, op. 53, no. 4*

Adagio

The sense of motion forward to the next down-beat, imparted by the anacrusis, seems to be continually present in melodies possessing unmistakable rhythmic vitality, such as those of J. S. Bach. It is as though each down-beat serves in turn as a springboard for the start of another anacrusis, ever renewing the rhythmic life of the melody.

In some phrases which start with an anacrusis this is preceded by a rest taking the place of a down-beat, and this rest is actually felt to be a necessary part of the rhythm of the phrase. Two such phrase beginnings are given below. A comparison of these with the phrase by Mendelssohn in example 44 will demonstrate the principle of a rest serving as the first down-beat. The notes following the rest constitute an anacrusis to the next down-beat, and in the case of the Mozart example a remarkably long one.

EX. 45. Mozart—*Flute Concerto, K. 313*

EX. 46. Handel—*Concerto Grosso no. 10*

Our musical notation is admittedly inadequate in the indication of rhythm. The use of bar-lines is often misleading as to the distribution of strong beats and as to whether these are up-beats or down-beats. The interpretation of rhythm is nearly always open to differences of opinion. Even in as well known a passage as the following quotation from a Beethoven sonata the question arises whether it should be played so as to explain the meter, by accenting the first D and then the A in the next measure, or whether the motive of two sixteenths and an eighth should be given the same rhythm consistently throughout. In a broader view, it appears that the only rhythmically strong tone here is the quarter note D, and that all the initial rising scale acts as anacrusis to the D as down-beat.

EX. 47. Beethoven—*Sonata, op. 14, no. 2*

As suggested by example 47, not single measures but whole melodic units, or phrases, should serve as the basis for the interpretation of melodic rhythm. One should first find the chief point, or points, of stress, then those of secondary importance, and note the position and relation of these points in reference to the phrase as a whole.

EX. 48. Beethoven—*Symphony no. 1*

Rhythmically, the B-flat in the next to last measure is doubtless the strongest tone in this melody. The first three bars are preceded by strong up-beats, making the three secondary strong beats C, F, and A. All the staccato notes are weak and of equal stress. Leading up to the strongest tone B-flat there is an anacrusis of four notes. It is necessary to remark that the qualifications strong and weak in rhythm do not mean loud and soft. The entire phrase remains in the nuance *pianissimo*.

In the following example there is no coincidence between first beats of the meter and strong beats of the melody. It is nevertheless essential that the choice of measure should indicate to the player the down-beat quality of the first E-flat. The meaning of the phrase would be radically altered if the first note were conceived as an up-beat, with down-beat on the second note, B-flat.

EX. 49. J. S. Bach—*Well-tempered Clavier, I, Fugue no. 8*

DISTRIBUTION OF MELODIC ACTIVITY

Considerations of unity and variety influence the distribution of long and short note values in a well balanced line. In this respect the melodic line by Bach shown below is admirably disposed. The rhythmic patterns of smaller units are continually varied (there are only two measures whose rhythmic patterns occur twice), and at the same time the

differences are not so marked that there is any weakening of the unity
of the phrase.

EX. 50. J. S. Bach—*The Art of Fugue, Contrapunctus V*

Although the question of unity and variety is of necessity closely related to that of motive structure to be taken up later, much can be
learned through observing and imitating the patterns made by the distribution of short and long time values. The following example shows
well balanced distribution.

EX. 51. Bruckner—*Symphony no. 7*

Not all lines are as finely planned rhythmically as these. On the other
hand it should be remembered that various other factors may influence
the method of distribution of melodic activity. For instance, a composer
may deliberately put all the activity into the second half of the melody,
emphasizing the idea of antecedent and consequent parts of the phrase.

EX. 52. J. S. Bach—*Three-part Invention no. 13*

Rhythmic activity is sometimes limited to constant repetition of some rhythmic motive, with more emphasis on unity and the melodic curve than on variety of rhythm.

EX. 53. Brahms—*Intermezzo, op. 117, no. 3*

Andante con moto

Occasionally, lines are constructed entirely of notes of equal time value. This type of line is most often used in combination with other lines, or it is a variation of some melody previously heard, although in the example below it is entirely self-sufficient and appropriate to the style.

EX. 54. Handel—*Suite for Harpsichord* from (*Klavierbuch aus der Jugendzeit*)

Courante

EXERCISES

1. Construct experimental melodic lines (a) with strong beats in agreement with the meter, (b) with strong beats in disagreement with the meter, (c) with a mixture of these two effects.

2. Construct a phrase illustrating the principle of strong up-beat followed by weak down-beat.

3. Construct a phrase in which accents are produced by melodic skip and by appoggiatura.

4. Construct a phrase beginning with a long anacrusis.

5. Derive rhythmic patterns from various melodies found in musical literature and construct phrases on these rhythmic patterns, using different melodic curves. This should be done with the objective of learning more about the example studied, rather than of obtaining fine musical results in the form of new melodies.

6. Construct phrases on the following rhythmic patterns, using various types of melodic curves, with different pitch locations.

(a) (from Beethoven—*Symphony no. 3*)

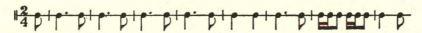

(b) (from Chopin—*Mazurka, op. 63, no. 2*)

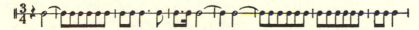

(c) (from Bach—*The Art of Fugue, Contrapunctus I*)

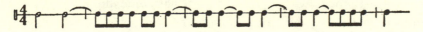

CHAPTER THREE

THE HARMONIC BASIS

T HE process of creating melody, during the period we are now considering, is hardly to be separated from that of creating harmony. Not only is it extremely rare that a composer first writes a melodic phrase without reference to its harmonic background, but melodies are most commonly derived from harmonic patterns chosen in advance.

Evidence to support this view lies in the striking similarity noticeable in the harmonic organization of so many melodies composed over a period of two centuries. To a lesser degree, this similarity still exists in much music of the twentieth century, even while composers have consciously sought to avoid stereotyped patterns. Given our long heritage of associating melody with harmony, it is doubtful whether one can hear melody today without sensing some harmonic implications, like or unlike those in the mind of the composer.

The harmony on which the melody is based, or from which it is derived, may not always be evident to the hearer if the melody is first heard unaccompanied. Every melody can be given a different harmonization from that with which it was created. The new harmony may even suggest a new meaning for the melody, especially in its rhythmic interpretation.

EX. 55

G: IV   I   V   II   V of VI

In the first instance shown above, the B in the upper voice sounds rhythmically weak, whereas in the second arrangement B is heard as a strong tone because of its relation to the harmony.

One may assume that a composer presents his melody accompanied by the harmonic background originally created with it, and that the meaning of both elements is, musically speaking, what he intended. As a matter of fact, the creative process is one of give and take, both melody and harmony undergoing changes until the final result acceptable to the composer is arrived at.

To the student, seeking a knowledge of the practice of composers through the method of retracing their constructive procedures, it should be emphasized that even while concentrating on counterpoint and the linear aspect of music, he should see to it that the harmony is well made, in his own mind at least. Root movements are important to the fundamental structure of the phrase, quite apart from the forms of the chords employed on these roots. The tonality must be sound at all times, although modulation may be freely used. The modes are limited to major and minor, but occasional experimentation with other scales will prove beneficial, especially to advanced students. Harmonic analysis should be shown by symbols with all exercises.

Since theoretical practice in the use of symbols identifying chords differs widely, these two statements of principle are needed to make clear the procedure followed in this book:

(a) Roman numerals identify the scale degree acting as root of the chord, whether or not the root is present in one of the voices. They do not indicate the form of the chord constructed on that root. For example, D:I means any chord whose root is the tonic of the key of D, major or minor.

(b) Arabic numerals are combined with Roman numerals for the purpose of explaining the form of the chord by indicating intervals between the bass note and other voices. These intervals are understood to be diatonic unless chromatic change is shown by placing an accidental beside the number. This use of Arabic numerals is similar to that found in eighteenth century figured bass parts. Further details will have been learned in the study of harmony.

CHORD-LINE MELODY

Some melodies are made wholly or in large part from tones of the harmony.

EX. 56. Beethoven—*Violin Concerto*

EX. 57. Handel—*Water Music*

This type of line possesses little independence relative to the harmonic background and in so far may be said to be less contrapuntal than other types. Any contrapuntal effect it may have is caused by differences between the melodic and harmonic rhythms.

CHROMATICISM

Various reasons can be advanced to explain why a certain melody does not suggest its harmony to the hearer. These include the harmonic versatility of long held tones, the absence of chord outlines, the presence of nonharmonic tones, and the use of chromaticism, although the last two conditions may on occasion imply definite harmony. Certainly the melody of the following example when played alone gives but slight hint of the harmony written by the composer.

EX. 58. Wagner—*Parsifal*

There are four ways to account for the presence of chromatic tones in the melody, given the harmonic style of the period we are studying. They may occur as factors in secondary dominant harmony, as factors in altered chords, as chromatic nonharmonic tones, or as scale degrees in an interchange of major and minor modes.

A certain amount of chromaticism is common to the period. The fugal style of Johann Sebastian Bach points to an advanced degree of freedom in this respect. In harmony, chromaticism means the use of all secondary dominants (and some subdominants), including the diminished seventh chords; altered chords such as the Neapolitan sixth, the raised supertonic and submediant, and even occasionally the augmented sixth; chromatically altered passing tones, appoggiature, etc.; and complete mixture of major and minor modes on the same tonic.

In general, chromatic alteration creates tendency tones, or adds to the tendency a tone already has. A tone chromatically raised acquires thereby a tendency to continue upward, whereas a lowered tone is given a downward tendency. Thus the forward motion of the music is aided by chromaticism, although too much melodic movement by half-steps is likely to impair the individuality and strength of the melodic lines.

DISSONANCE

Chromaticism is allied to dissonance, since both contribute to the forward motion of music. Dissonance, however, is more typically a contrapuntal element, involving as it does the principle of disagreement between ingredients of the texture.

HARMONIC DISSONANCE

Considering the single melodic line and its harmony, we find dissonance used in two different ways, as harmonic dissonance or as contrapuntal dissonance. In harmonic dissonance the dissonant tone is regarded as a factor in a dissonant chord, and is so treated.

EX. 59. Mozart—*Fantasia, K. 475*

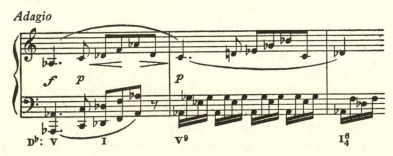

The G-flat and B-flat in the right-hand part (second measure) are clearly chord members in a dominant ninth chord. While the G may be said to have its resolution in the left-hand part, the ninth has no resolution at all.

EX. 60. J. S. Bach—*Three-part Invention no. 10*

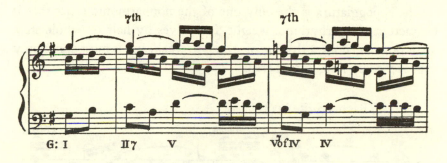

In this example are seen two harmonic dissonances, each appearing as a chordal seventh. Both receive proper contrapuntal resolution but they are none the less true harmonic factors.

CONTRAPUNTAL DISSONANCE

Contrapuntal dissonance is created by melodic nonharmonic tones. These are distinguished by their disagreement with the harmony against which they sound and so they are real contrapuntal tones.

Harmonic dissonances may be treated as contrapuntal dissonances and it will be recalled from the study of harmony that many of them are regularly treated as such. For instance, the seventh of the subdominant seventh chord may be analyzed nearly always as an appoggiatura or suspension, and most ninth, eleventh, and thirteenth chords are readily explained as simpler chords upon which nonharmonic tones have been superposed.

In the study of counterpoint, considerable attention should be given to recognizing the true melodic character of these so-called nonharmonic tones. We may accept the term nonharmonic, since such tones are ordinarily not members of the accompanying harmony, but their purely melodic significance can hardly be overemphasized. As a group they are sometimes called nonessential tones, a characterization which is true only as far as harmony is concerned. Melodically these tones are the opposite of nonessential, often being themselves the distinctive features of individual melodies.

THE APPOGGIATURA

The appoggiatura is the only one of the nonharmonic tones that is characterized by rhythmic weight. It resolves by half or whole step, up or down, making a rhythm of strong to weak, and is most commonly approached by skip, unprepared.

EX. 61. J. S. Bach—*Suite in D*

The rhythmic stress of the appoggiatura is heightened if its time value is long compared to the notes preceding or following it. In the example below, the A-sharp and E-sharp are strong tones melodically because of their length and their introduction by skip. They are also chromatic appoggiature, raised tones with upward tendency.

EX. 62. Brahms—*Symphony no. 2*

It is not necessary that the rhythmic weight of the appoggiatura be so marked as to be dynamically accented. The stress may be a matter of subtle rhythmic feeling rather than of accentuation.

EX. 63. Tchaikowsky—*Symphony no. 4*

This rhythmic subtlety is illustrated by the following example showing the distinction between the passing tone and the appoggiatura approached by step and continuing in the same direction.

EX. 64. Franck—*Quintet*

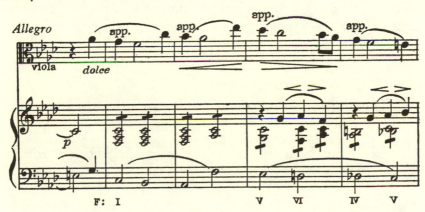

One has only to imagine this melody as it would be played with the bar moved to the left by the value of a quarter-note (example 65) to realize that the leaning quality (Italian, *appoggiare*, to lean) would then disappear and the G, B-flat, and D-flat, would become passing tones. In other words, there is in the appoggiatura a certain down-beat quality even when its rhythmic weight is but slightly stressed, if at all.

EX. 65

The appoggiatura may be prepared by the same tone in the preceding chord. The note of preparation is usually given a shorter time value than the appoggiatura, in order to preserve the rhythmic stress of the latter.

EX. 66. J. S. Bach—*Sonata no. 1, for Violin Alone*

Similar to the above, rhythmically, is the common preparation of the appoggiatura by an anticipation, itself a nonharmonic tone.

EX. 67. Weber—*Euryanthe, Overture*

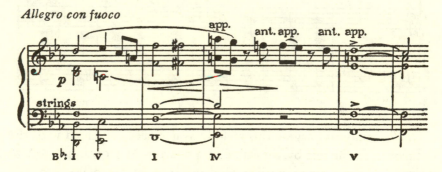

THE PASSING TONE

Passing tones, moving by whole or half step, diatonic or chromatic, in one direction, are used to continue scalewise motion in the melodic line. They are always of weak rhythmic quantity, even when occurring on the first beat of the measure.

EX. 68. Carl Philipp Emanuel Bach—*Sonata no. 4*

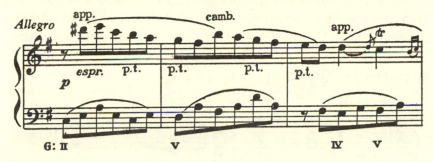

A comparison of the above example with example 64 is useful to show the difference between the appoggiatura and the passing tone on the beat. The appoggiatura has the feeling of rhythmic weight, whereas the passing tone merely passes without stress no matter where it occurs.

The following example by Beethoven contains numerous passing tones, some falling on beats and some not, but all are unaccented. In the first measure, right hand, third to fourth beats, two passing tones are necessary to fill in the interval of a fourth between chord tones. Notice the dissonant combination of notes on the first beat of the second measure. In measure three are two chromatic passing tones, A-sharp and F-double sharp.

EX. 69. Beethoven—*Sonata for Piano and Violoncello, op. 69*

Occasionally a phrase starts with an anacrusis of one note which has the external appearance of an appoggiatura but which is not stressed. Such a tone as the E-natural in the example below may sound most like a passing tone with missing antecedent, here sounded in another voice.

EX. 70. Haydn—*Quartet, op. 76, no. 4*

Examples are numerous of the common type of passing tone. Measure four of the same Haydn excerpt contains three: A, G, and E-flat.

THE SUSPENSION

In its commonest and most characteristic form, the suspension is prepared by a note of comparatively long time value which is tied over the bar and which resolves on an important metric division of the measure.

EX. 71. Haydn—*Oxford Symphony*

To be a true suspension in the harmonic sense, the tone suspended (tied over) must at the point of suspension become a tone foreign to the harmony, or let us say the harmony must change and become foreign to the tone. Evidently any tied-over note is a suspension in the purely melodic sense, but we are using the term suspension in its accepted meaning as a nonharmonic tone.

The suspension is the most contrapuntal of the nonharmonic tones since it avoids rhythmic stress at a point where other voices and the harmonic rhythm are likely to give a down-beat. Thus a moment of disagreement between the melodic and harmonic rhythms results from the use of a suspension. This dissonance is usually prolonged at least a whole beat, although suspensions of shorter duration are also employed.

EX. 72. Mozart—*Symphony, K. 504*

If the preparation of the suspension is short we get rather the impression of an appoggiatura tied to its anticipation.

EX. 73. Beethoven—*Sonata, op. 90*

Here the F-sharp in the bass and the accented G in the upper voice sound like anticipated appoggiature. Both tones might also be analyzed

as harmonic dissonances, making a submediant seventh chord in measure two and a dominant ninth chord in the last measure.

Suspensions may be resolved upward, even though the tone may not
in itself have an upward tendency. Such a resolution follows more naturally, of course, in the case of suspended leading tones, or chromatically raised tones. In all other cases it must be regarded as exceptional.

EX. 74. Schumann—*Carnaval*

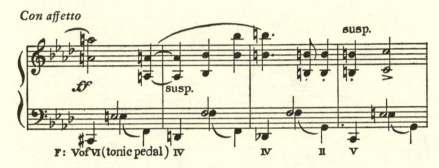

In the fourth measure of this example the B-natural is evidently unaccented, so it does not have the rhythm of an anticipated appoggiatura.
It is similar to the suspension two measures before, except that the repeated notes take the place of the longer held note.

The resolution of the suspension may be delayed so that it resolves
into a different harmony from that against which it sounded. This is
the contrapuntal origin of many seventh, ninth, eleventh, and thirteenth chord effects. In the following case, the suspension E has for its
resolution D, the root of a tonic triad. When the resolution takes place,
however, the harmony has changed so that the D is now the third in a
triad on the sixth degree. The tonic triad is at no point heard as such,
so that it is possible to describe the harmonic effect on the first beat
of the second measure as a tonic ninth chord, with E as a ninth. Needless to say, the melodic interpretation of E as a nonharmonic tone is
more in keeping with our present interest in counterpoint as a combination of melodic lines.

EX. 75. J. S. Bach—*Allabreve for Organ*

The tone prolonged to make the suspension is as a rule a factor of the harmony. Exceptionally, this tone is nonharmonic, so that one might, without being entirely illogical, speak for instance of a suspended passing tone, like the C in the second measure of the example below.

EX. 76. J. S. Bach—*The Art of Fugue, Contrapunctus 1*

THE ANTICIPATION

The name of the anticipation explains its function. Anticipations are necessarily shorter in time value than the tone anticipated, if their true character and rhythm are to be kept. This does not preclude a certain expressive importance being given the anticipation, as in many familiar classic cadential formulae.

EX. 77. J. S. Bach—*Organ Fugue in B Minor*

In the following example the anticipations are of equal time value to the tones anticipated and are of considerable significance in the melodic expression. It is through them that tension seems to be built up in this melody until the cadential measures are reached. This illustration provides convincing evidence of the essential quality of nonharmonic tones.

EX. 78. Johann Christian Bach—*Concerto no. 1 for Harpsichord and String Orchestra*

Quite a different effect comes from tying the anticipation to the note anticipated. In this case the accent shifts to the anticipation and there results a somewhat breathless type of syncopation.

EX. 79. J. S. Bach—*Well-tempered Clavier, I, Prelude no. 13*

THE AUXILIARY

The auxiliary is an ornament to a single tone, leaving that tone by whole or half step and returning to it. It may be above or below the main note. The harmony does not necessarily remain the same throughout this process.

EX. 80. Schubert—*Quintet, op. 163*

ÉCHAPPÉE AND CAMBIATA

A melodic movement of a second is often varied by the interpolation of a third tone outside the line of movement. The échappée leaves the first tone by step and returns by skip of a third to the tone of destination; the cambiata is introduced by skip of a third from the first tone and resolves into the final tone by step. Both are weak rhythmically.

EX. 81

By extension of this principle of ornamentation of a fundamental melodic movement, the échappée sometimes moves over a skip larger than a third.

EX. 82. Liszt—*Les Préludes*

Further freedom in the use of this resource allows the skip to be made in the same direction as the approach to the échappée, giving the impression of a passing tone moving by more than a second.

EX. 83. Chopin—*Prelude, op. 28, no. 1*

In the case of the cambiata it is the interval of approach that may sometimes be larger than a third. The tone remains weak in rhythm, so it is not to be confused with the appoggiatura.

EX. 84. Mendelssohn—*Midsummer Night's Dream, Intermezzo*

Like the échappée, the cambiata may be approached and left without change of direction, with the same passing tone impression.

EX. 85. Handel—*Concerto Grosso no. 5*

Echappée and cambiata combine to form the effect commonly called double auxiliary, or changing-tones, as in the first measure of the following example.

EX. 86. Haydn—*Sonata no. 3*

ORNAMENTAL RESOLUTION

The melodic ornamentation shown by the last four illustrations is frequently employed in connection with the resolution of any dissonance. Example 86 shows, in the second measure, an appoggiatura B-natural resolving to C, the resolution ornamented by the interpolated cambiata D. In the two examples below are seen some of the various ornamental resolutions of suspensions. The tone interpolated between the dissonance and its note of resolution may be an échappée, cambiata, or chord tone, or there may be a group of interpolated tones.

EX. 87. J. S. Bach—*Well-tempered Clavier, I, Prelude no. 13*

EX. 88. J. S. Bach—*Italian Concerto*

It is recommended that the entire second movement of Bach's Italian Concerto, from which the above excerpt is taken, be studied in detail from the point of view of melodic analysis, especially for the great freedom and flexibility it shows in the use of these nonharmonic tones. There probably exists no finer example of a long sustained expressive line, written in counterpoint to a steadily moving harmonic background.

EXERCISES

Since we are interested primarily in an element of music that is not to be found separate from other elements, namely counterpoint, it is advisable and even necessary to exaggerate that element in written studies. Hence the student is urged to refrain from emphasis on harmonic effects as such. To obtain more benefits from contrapuntal studies, the use of harmonic dissonance and chromatic chords should be kept to a minimum.

1. On each of the following harmonic patterns construct at least three different melodic lines. Use various types of melodic curve and give attention to the organization of melodic rhythm. Employ non-harmonic tones. Write only the melody, not the bass, nor the suggested chords. The lines should be at least six measures long, preferably longer. The chords may be distributed over the measures in any way, provided their sequence as given is preserved.

(a) E-flat major: V–VI–IV–I–IV–V–III–VI–II–V–I
(b) A minor: I–V–I–IV–II–V–VI–IV–II–V–I
(c) C (mode optional): I–IV–I–VI–VofV–V–VofVI–IV–V
(d) D (mode mixed): IV–V–VI–II–VofVI–VI–VofV–V–I–IV–I

2. Make five different versions of the two basic melodic lines below. In each version vary the basic line by the application of one of the ornamental melodic devices as many times as it can be applied, using the following schedule:

version *a*, appoggiatura   version *d*, échappée and cambiata
version *b*, suspension   version *e*, suspension with ornamental
version *c*, auxiliary   resolution

Indicate by symbols the harmony understood. It need not be the same for all five versions.

CHAPTER FOUR

HARMONIC RHYTHM

THE harmonic background of the phrase supplies not only tonal support and color, but it also makes an important contribution of a rhythmic nature to the total effect. A rhythmic pattern is formed by the root changes in the harmony, consisting of various time values with strong and weak progressions. This pattern of the harmonic rhythm can be transcribed with reasonable accuracy, and it will be seen to bear a contrapuntal relationship to the melodic line. That is to say, it will be noticed that elements of agreement and disagreement exist between the two rhythmic organizations, melodic and harmonic. Harmonic rhythm is therefore a necessary aspect of the study of counterpoint.

This counterpoint of rhythms is perhaps most easily perceived when the root changes succeed one another with steady regularity while the melodic rhythm follows a more or less flexible pattern of strong and weak values. In the example shown below, not only are the harmonic changes alike in time, but they are likewise similar in that they are all what we call strong progressions. With but two exceptions the root movements are by ascending fourths.

EX. 89. J. S. Bach—*Well-tempered Clavier, II, Fugue no. 14*

F#: I   V   I   IV   V of III III   VI   II   V   I   II   V

harmonic rhythm:

The situation may be reversed, with the regular pulse recurring in the melody, against a flexible harmonic rhythm. This flexibility is due to variations in time quantities and variations in the relative strength of the root progressions, as in the following, by Brahms. In the third full measure the dominant harmony receives stress, by virtue of the approach from IV. In like manner the next chord, I, is made a strong harmony. These two progressions, IV–V and V–I, are the only strong root changes in the phrase.

EX. 90. Brahms—*Intermezzo, op. 116, no. 6*

Andantino teneramente

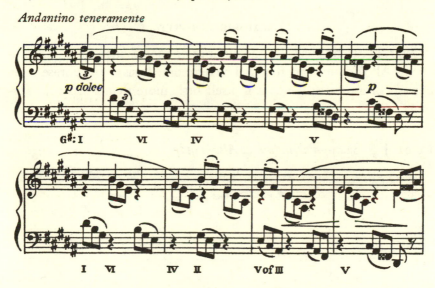

harmonic rhythm:

It is common in well organized music for both the melodic and harmonic rhythms to show some degree of flexibility.

EX. 91. Beethoven—*Quartet, op. 18, no. 1*

harmonic rhythm:

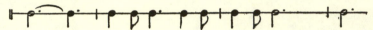

HARMONIC ACTIVITY

No rule can be given for the number of root changes in a phrase of music. All variations are found. The harmonic basis of the phrase often consists of a pattern which is in itself little more than a cadential formula.

EX. 92. J. S. Bach—*Partita no. 4, Allemande*

harmonic rhythm:

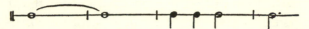

The contrapuntal quality of the music is less pronounced if the phrase contains a large number of root changes. Emphasis is then rather on the harmony than on the melodic threads. Dissonances appear as harmonic dissonances and the hearer is more conscious of seventh and ninth chords than of suspensions and other contrapuntal effects. It is also to be observed that rapid succession of root changes tends to hold back the tempo, suggesting that much harmonic activity is not appropriate to fast moving music.

EX. 93. J. S. Bach—*Well-tempered Clavier, I, Prelude no. 24*

D: VI   III   II · V   I   VI   IV   II   V   VI   II   V   I

harmonic rhythm:

METRIC RELATIONSHIPS

Although meter does not contribute rhythm, the relations between the pulse implied by regular divisions and what is actually heard, i. e. the combination of melodic with harmonic rhythm, are of great importance in any study of the rhythmic texture of music.

It is indisputable that most music has a regularly recurring pulse, as demonstrated by the fact that equal measures can be applied to it and fit very well indeed. This regularity, far from being a defect, proves to be an excellent means of setting off the great variety of rhythmic resource in melody and harmony, a foil against which flexibility is all the more effective.

The uneven pulses found in both old and new music are, of course, exceptions to this rule. The reader is reminded that in the present study we are interested primarily in the clarification of the common practice of composers over a certain general historical period, hence the definiteness of the foregoing remarks.

When the down-beats of both melodic and harmonic rhythms coincide with the first beats of the meter, purely contrapuntal interest is at a minimum.

EX. 94. Schubert—*Sonatina for Violin and Piano, op. 137, no. 3*

harmonic rhythm:

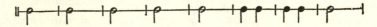

A more contrapuntal quality is present if the strong beats of the melodic rhythm do not coincide with first beats of the measures. Very often in such cases the metric divisions are explained to the hearer by the harmonic rhythm, the root changes coinciding with the bar-lines of the meter, as in example 95.

In example 96, it is this agreement between meter and harmonic rhythm which makes evident the peculiar syncopation of the melody.

EX. 95. Chopin—*Mazurka, op. 63, no. 2*

harmonic rhythm:

EX. 96. Schumann—*Kinderscenen, op. 15, no. 10*

harmonic rhythm:

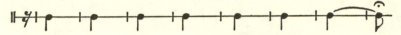

The melody, if heard unaccompanied, would certainly sound this way:

EX. 97

If melodic and harmonic rhythms agree in their strong beats, but do not agree with the metric pulse, the hearer is momentarily unaware of the position of the written bar-line and he may unconsciously adopt some other metric division. Rediscovery of the fundamental metric pulse gives added rhythmic interest, although if it is kept hidden for too long a time the effect may be that of an actual shift of the bar-line, or pulse. At what point this happens will depend on the sensitivities of the individual hearer, and especially on his familiarity with the particular piece of music. One is quite likely to retain the pulse mentally on hearing a repetition of the phrase, or if the music has been continuing for some time without variation of meter.

The Mozart example below is quite simple in this respect, whereas the Bach excerpt raises the question whether the sound is not as though the bar-line were placed one eighth-note later, especially since the root movements are all strong progressions.

EX. 98. Mozart—*Concerto for Two Pianos, K. 365*

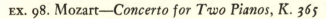

harmonic rhythm:

EX. 99. J. S. Bach—*Well-tempered Clavier, I, Prelude no. 22*

F: VI II   V   III   I II   VI

harmonic rhythm:

In example 100, the harmonic rhythm is clear enough to the player, but since it is the start of a movement and the listener has no previously defined pulse to help him, the probability is that the syncopated melodic rhythms will prevent his discovering the position of the down-beats and the root changes until the cadence is reached. When the same phrase returns later in the piece no such ambiguity will be experienced, the metric pulse being well established. There will be, however, the added interest of a counterpoint of rhythms, one of which the hearer knows but does not hear.

EX. 100. Haydn—*Sonata no. 12*

Eb: V I   V   IV I   II I   V   IV

harmonic rhythm:

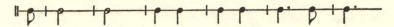

When there is lack of coincidence among all three elements, melodic rhythm, harmonic rhythm, and meter, the sense of the metric pulse is lost to the hearer. In this comparatively unusual situation, it is often possible to apply a new meter to the music. The harmonic rhythm of the following example could, for instance, be barred in a meter of four-four, starting with the second quarter of the first measure. The composer's intention, however, is undoubtedly to create this momentary confusion, which gets straightened out at the cadence by obvious return to the original metric pulse.

EX. 101. Haydn—*Quartet, op. 20, no. 4*

harmonic rhythm:

STATIC HARMONY

Absence of root change means absence of harmonic rhythm. The metric pulse is in this case suggested, if so desired, by the melodic rhythm. The effect of this static harmony is of relaxation and immobility.

EX. 102. Beethoven—*Quartet, op. 59, no. 1*

harmonic rhythm:

The meter of the above could, of course, be shown by giving to the upper parts accents which they do not possess. Such accents would not, however, be accents of the harmonic rhythm, which occur only through root change.

Some static quality is given to the harmony by the use of the pedal point, although the effect is not truly static harmony. The pedal imparts a sense of not moving, but the root changes of the harmonies above are clearly felt, and when the chord is dissonant to the pedal tone, a harmonic accent is ordinarily the result.

EX. 103. Mozart—*Symphony, K. 504*

harmonic rhythm:

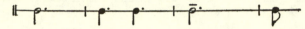

EXERCISES

1. Construct melodic lines according to these specifications:
   - (a) The strong beats of the harmonic rhythm coincide with the metric pulse, but not with the strong beats of the melodic rhythm.
   - (b) The strong beats of harmonic and melodic rhythms coincide, but do not agree with first beats of the metric pulse.
   - (c) The strong beats of the harmonic rhythm do not coincide with those of the melodic rhythm, and both are at variance with the first beats of the metric pulse.

2. Construct melodic lines on the following patterns of harmonic rhythm:

   (a)

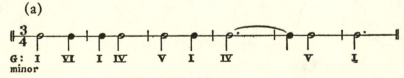

   (b)

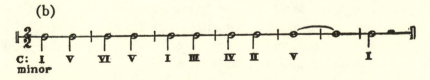

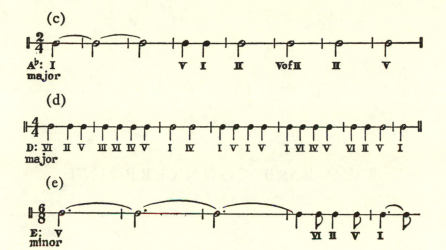

CHAPTER FIVE

⇶⇷

TWO-PART COUNTERPOINT

THE outstanding characteristics presented by the combination of two melodic lines, in ideal form, are independence of melodic curve, independence of rhythmic stress, and balance of rhythmic activity. Although the individuality of each line is marked in these respects, both are ordinarily based on the same harmonic background and they are not widely divergent in style or thematic content.

EX. 104. J. S. Bach—*Well-tempered Clavier, I, Fugue no. 4*

EX. 105. J. S. Bach—*The Art of Fugue, Contrapunctus XIV*

The melodic lines in these examples stand on a level of equality in musical significance and the pairs are rhythmically well balanced. Melodic equality is not, however, a necessary attribute of two-part counterpoint in all of its uses. The bass line which accompanies a melody is very often organized in contrapuntal, although subordinate, relationship to the upper voice, and it has its own melodic curve together with some independence of rhythm.

EX. 106. Beethoven—*Symphony no. 5*

The subordinate melodic bass sometimes proceeds in steadily moving notes of equal value so that it is lacking in rhythmic pattern, while retaining its contrapuntal melodic curve. The following example includes figures indicating the harmony to be filled in by the harpsichord player, but the two parts are in themselves harmonically sufficient.

EX. 107. Handel—*Sonata, op. 1, no. 6, for Oboe with Figured Bass*

Application of the principle demonstrated above, that of a contrapuntal part progressing in notes always of the same time value, is not confined to bass lines. The process is used to form arabesque-like counterpoint against the principal melody, either above or below it.

EX. 108. Mozart—*Sonata, K. 498a*

The contrapuntal quality of lines of this type depends on the excellence of the curve thus formed, the degree of contrast noticeable between the two melodic curves, and the amount of dissonance created by the two voices, especially on important beats. In the examples shown, nos. 108 and 109, we should rate the lines fairly high on the first two points but rather low on the third.

EX. 109. Beethoven—*Sonata, op. 110*

Good two-part counterpoint is self-sufficient harmonically and so it does not need the support of other parts to explain its harmony, although some intervals, like the third, may be suggestive of more than one harmonic root. It may be superposed on a harmonic background or accompaniment without affecting its validity as two-part counterpoint, a common procedure in orchestral writing.

By means of accompanying harmony, the harmonic implication of the counterpoint can be given a new and unexpected interpretation, as in the example below. In the second measure the change to a harmony of VI is brought about solely through the introduction of the A in the accompaniment.

EX. 110. Chopin—*Etude, op. 25, no. 7*

An important feature of independence of the melodic curves is that the high points or peaks of the curves do not arrive at the same moment. In the following illustration each line has two important high points. Those in the lower part are reached about a measure sooner than those in the upper voice.

EX. 111. Beethoven—*Sonata for Violin and Piano, op. 30, no. 1*

In example 112 the upper voice reaches its peak before the lower despite the fact that the latter began first. The high points are strongly accented in both parts.

EX. 112. J. S. Bach—*Organ Fugue in C Minor*

A different situation is seen in the next example. Here the upper voice shows a curve which has four secondary peaks on G and one principle high point, A, in the third measure. The bass, on the other hand, starts with its peak, D, and gradually descends. In performance, one is quite distinctly aware of the increasing space between the two lines, and the low A-sharp is heard as a primary objective of the lower melody.

EX. 113. C. P. E. Bach—*Concerto in D Major*

Insufficiency in rhythmic independence can be offset to a certain extent by opposition of the melodic curves. The lines in the short excerpt below follow curves which may be said to be the reverse of each other, this being about the only contrapuntal attribute discernible in the passage.

EX. 114. Beethoven—*Sonata, op. 13*

When rhythmic independence is lacking and the melodic curves are similar, the contrapuntal quality of the two-part writing is greatly reduced. In the following example by Bach, the momentary bits of contrary motion are not enough to counteract the almost complete interdependence of the lines.

It is well at this point to remind the reader that to point out a greater or lesser degree of contrapuntal quality in a piece of music is not to evaluate its success as music. As stated at the outset of these studies, all music is not contrapuntal, and the contrapuntal element in music is an extremely variable quantity. Our purpose here must be the analytical and objective examination of that element, in all its aspects, as used by composers.

EX. 115. J. S. Bach—*Organ Fugue in C Minor*

Varying the rhythmic activity throughout the phrase, and distributing this activity between the voices lends a more contrapuntal feeling to two lines whose curves are so similar as to be practically identical (example 116). Here the fundamental movement is in parallel thirds and sixths, but the melodic rhythms are varied by syncopation and the introduction of passing tones. The two parts remain but slightly independent notwithstanding.

EX. 116. Brahms—*Symphony no. 1*

The following phrase is more contrapuntal in feeling because the fundamental curves are not as nearly parallel as in the Brahms example, and the alternation in rhythmic activity causes the listener's attention to pass back and forth between the voices. In less skilful hands such rhythmic alternation may become a mannerism devoid of contrapuntal interest. The student should note carefully the slight variations made by Beethoven in the answering voice, and how effective these are in bringing a subtle variety to the unity of this rhythmic device.

EX. 117. Beethoven—*Quartet, op. 127*

Sometimes one line is simply a variation of the other. This effect, shown in the example below, must not be mistaken for real counterpoint. The two melodies possess practically no independence.

EX. 118. Brahms—*Symphony no. 2*

In most instances the underlying pulse of the two lines is the same. A special use of counterpoint is in the combination of two melodies when one is moving to a slower pulse than the other. The following excerpt shows two different themes combined. Each theme has been heard previously so that each is readily recognized. The lower voice not only moves with a pulse twice as slow as the upper voice, but its metric grouping is ternary in contrast to the binary pulse of the upper melody and of the pizzicato accompaniment, here omitted.

EX. 119. Berlioz—*Harold in Italy*

In fugal writing the subject is on occasion combined with itself in augmentation, that is in notes twice as long. The rhythmic impression is not unlike that of seeing two persons walking together, one taking a single step to the other's two.

EX. 120. J. S. Bach—*The Art of Fugue, Contrapunctus VII*

The subject appears in the upper voice in inverted form, as well as in augmentation.

CROSSING OF VOICES

In two-part writing the voices may cross quite freely, as long as the integrity of each melodic curve is maintained and each voice is balanced on its own pitch location. Hence the voices ought not to remain crossed for too long, so that what began as the lower part becomes identified as the upper.

Unisons of short duration frequently occur. Usually at least one of the voices involved in the unison is at the moment weak in rhythmic stress. Care is nearly always taken not to approach a unison from an interval of a second, when the tone approached is sustained through both intervals.

EX. 121. Treatment of Unisons

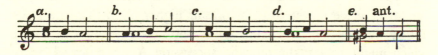

In *a* the holding tone A is approached from the interval of a second. This effect is usually avoided, no doubt on account of its lack of acoustical clarity. To the ear, the moving voice seems to disappear into the holding tone. On the other hand, leaving the unison by a second, as in *b,* is common practice, and both *c* and *d* are considered good approaches to the unison. In example *e*, often used in cadences, the case is somewhat changed by the fact that the A in this instance is not a holding tone.

Two-part counterpoint between two voices having the same pitch location will inevitably bring about crossing of the voices.

EX. 122. J. S. Bach—*Brandenburg Concerto no. 6*

The treatment of unisons in the above example, where the sixteenth-note groups occur, is rather exceptional, especially in the second of the two cases, in which an auxiliary tone, D, is used on a unison, E-flat. A difference in dynamic level between the two viola parts is necessary to distinguish the separate voices in performance.

Overlapping of the voices is fairly consistently avoided in contrapuntal writing. The effect is readily seen in the example given below. The parts do not cross but in the first combination shown the F of the lower voice moves to C, a tone of higher pitch than the A just left by the upper part. There results a possible ambiguity to the ear, which might follow the melodic succession A–C, indicated by the dotted line.

EX. 123. Overlapping Voices

PARALLEL MOTION

Contrary motion is naturally typical of counterpoint. Two voices moving in opposite directions are certainly independent melodically. It is when they move in similar motion that the desired contrapuntal quality of independence may be lost if care is not taken with certain intervals. One can deduce general rules of procedure in the case of parallel movement of the voices.

EX. 124. Consecutive Octaves and Fifths

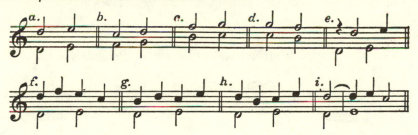

Two parts moving in octaves, as at *a*, are regarded as one part with a doubling at the octave. They are about as identical as they would be if they moved in unison. Octave doublings are widely employed in music, as almost any page will show, but parallel octaves are studiously avoided where independent contrapuntal voices are desired.

Parallel fifths are likewise avoided as having much the same effect on the dependence of the voices as parallel octaves, perhaps because the fifth is the next partial following the octave in the series of overtones on a given fundamental tone. By parallel fifths is meant perfect fifths, as at *b*. The example *c* shows a diminished fifth followed by a perfect fifth. This effect is not used in two-part writing, not because of the fifths but because of the unnatural resolution of the dissonant interval. The progression of perfect to diminished fifth, at *d*, is quite acceptable.

When the succession of octaves or fifths is complicated by the presence of other notes, or rhythmic differences, each case must be considered by itself on the basis of the amount of dependence existing between the two parts. As a variant of *a*, the simple syncopation shown at *e* certainly does not change matters much in this respect. At *f* the octaves fall simultaneously on the beats and the effect is almost as marked as at *a*. On the other hand, the formula at *g* seems to be open to question. It is used by Bach and others, and its acceptability appears to depend upon the rhythmic importance of the off beats. The progression at *h* is considered excellent because the intervening time value between the D and E in the upper voice is not shorter than the value of the D in the lower voice. Also commonly used is the ornamental resolution shown at *i*, in which the E in the upper voice is an échappée. In general the comparative rhythm of the two voices is the determining factor.

Following are examples of such consecutive octaves and fifths.

EX. 125. J. S. Bach—*Well-tempered Clavier, II, Prelude no. 10*

EX. 126. J. S. Bach—*Suite in D Major*

EX. 127. J. S. Bach—*Organ Fugue in C Major*

EX. 128. Haydn—*Symphony in D Major, no. 101*

EX. 129. Mozart—*Quartet, K. 589*

Voices moving in thirds and sixths are almost as dependent as those moving in octaves and fifths. The parts are not strictly parallel since there is some alternation between major and minor intervals. This procedure is a very common one but the effect is rather that of a single voice with harmonic doubling than that of a combination of contrapuntal lines.

EX. 130. Brahms—*Clarinet Quintet, op. 115*

Parts may occasionally move in consecutive dissonant intervals, seconds, fourths, sevenths, or ninths. In such combinations at least one nonharmonic tone will be involved, like the appoggiatura in the example below by Handel, and the passing-tone in example 132.

EX. 131. Handel—*Suite no. XV, Sarabande*

EX. 132. Mozart—*Sonata, K. 576*

DIRECT OCTAVES AND FIFTHS

Much has been written on the subject of the direct octave and direct fifth, otherwise known as hidden octaves and hidden fifths. What is meant is the interval of the octave or fifth, approached from another interval by similar motion. At least one of the voices moves by skip and the objection to the progression is based on the impression that the open interval of octave or fifth is unduly accentuated by this approach.

No rules regarding the treatment of direct octaves and fifths have been formulated which are substantiated by the practice of composers. The present writer believes that, rather than learn to follow a set of invented rules, the student should strive through study and analysis to develop powers of discrimination as to the degree of independence and individuality in melodic lines used in combination. The overemphasis on certain intervals may be qualified by many different factors, the most important of these being the separate rhythmic quantities of the two lines. This is noticeable in the two following examples.

EX. 133. J. S. Bach—*Well-tempered Clavier, II, Fugue no. 2*

EX. 134. J. S. Bach—*Well-tempered Clavier, II, Fugue no. 5*

As a generality it is true that two contrapuntal parts rarely move by skip simultaneously in the same direction. The example below is, then, exceptional. It will be noticed that the effect underlined is one rather of harmony than of counterpoint.

EX. 135. J. S. Bach—*Well-tempered Clavier, I, Fugue no. 19*

If dissonant intervals are approached by similar motion, they tend to be overemphasized, in the manner of direct octaves and fifths. The same rhythmic conditions affect the relative prominence of these intervals.

EX. 136. J. S. Bach—*Organ Fugue in C Major*

It should be apparent that the accentuation of the dissonant intervals in measure two is softened by the circumstance that the factors of the intervals in question are of unequal rhythmic weight. The passing tones are weaker than the tones approached by skip.

In example 137 the first two notes in the upper part receive very strong emphasis from the manner of their introduction. The descending scale produces passing tones on all beats but these are without rhythmic stress, whereas the tones in the left-hand part are all stressed for one reason or another. Incidentally, it is worth noting that the chromatic auxiliary in the last two measures makes possible the sounding together of D-natural and the harmonic seventh, D-flat.

EX. 137. Beethoven—*Sonata, op. 2, no. 1*

HARMONIC RELATIONSHIPS

The employment in two-part counterpoint of the open intervals of octave and fifth gives strength to the texture as well as relief from the softness of thirds and sixths.

EX. 138. Mozart—*Sonata, K. 284*

Even the perfect fourth, a dissonant interval in two-part writing, can be similarly used.

EX. 139. Franck—*Quartet*

Dissonances are normally resolved, in accordance with the natural tendency of the dissonant tone, as learned in the study of harmony. Tendency tones are usually not doubled, since one of the voices would then be forced to move contrary to its tendency. Also, a dissonant interval does not resolve by similar motion to an octave or unison. Such progressions are completely lacking in melodic independence of the two parts.

EX. 140.

It is the tendency of augmented intervals to expand, that of diminished intervals to contract.

EX. 141

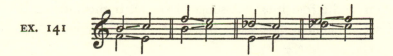

If the note of resolution of a dissonant tone sounds at the same time as the dissonance, it is not placed above the dissonance, nor is it placed so that it forms an interval of a second with the dissonant tone.

EX. 142

Of these three arrangements, *b* is customary, with the interval of a ninth resolving to the octave. In *a* the unison on C is approached from the interval of a second and the formula is therefore usually avoided. In *c* the interval of a seventh resolves unnaturally, the lower voice moving down to the octave. Mozart, however, did not regard this as bad practice, as can be seen from the following excerpt.

EX. 143. Mozart—*Quartet, K. 387*

THE SIX-FOUR CHORD

Detailed treatment of the six-four chord as a harmonic effect would be out of place in a study of counterpoint. Indeed, it will be recalled from the study of harmony that the six-four chord appears nearly always as a vertical sonority resulting from voice-leading, and so is rarely a chord in the true sense. The intervals of sixth and fourth are formed with the bass by nonharmonic tones in the upper parts.

Contrapuntally, consideration of the six-four chord means simply consideration of the fourth as a dissonant interval. If this interval is treated as a contrapuntal dissonance the question of six-four may be ignored.

Presence of the fifth of a triad in the lower voice sometimes gives the implication of a six-four chord. If this fifth is rhythmically a weak tone the implication is unimportant. On the other hand, there are to be found in the works of Bach and other composers a sufficient number of cases where the fifth of the chord, appearing in the bass, is stronger than the root, to suggest that this inversion is rather freely used when the successive intervals are sixth and third, and no interval of a fourth is actually present. The following example illustrates this point.

EX. 144. J. S. Bach—*The Art of Fugue, Contrapunctus VIII*

In the second and fourth measures of the example below, an interesting sonority, as of two superposed fourths, is made by the combination of a suspension with the root and fifth of the triad, the fifth being the lowest tone.

EX. 145. J. S. Bach—*Chorale Prelude, Allein Gott in der Höh' sei Ehr'*

CHROMATICISM

Both voices of the two-part texture may contain chromatic movement. It may be suggested, however, that the combination of chromatic progression in one part with diatonic movement in the other produces a stronger musical effect. From this standpoint compare the three following examples. Bach here accompanies the descending chromatic scale line by a completely diatonic part using the melodic minor scale forms. The Franck excerpt gives a feeling of simultaneous chromaticism in both voices, although they are not continuously chromatic. In the phrase by Beethoven, there is some chromatic movement in both parts, but this is distributed in such a way that two voices do not move chromatically at the same time.

EX. 146. J. S. Bach—*The Musical Offering, Ricercare*

EX. 147. Franck—*Prelude, Chorale, and Fugue*

EX. 148. Beethoven—*Quartet, op. 95*

Cross relation is freely used whenever it results from the employment of melodic and harmonic forms of the minor scale. In the example below, the A-natural in the upper voice is the seventh degree of the descending scale of B minor, whereas the A-sharp in the lower part is accounted for as the ascending leading-tone. This type of cross relation is of frequent occurrence.

EX. 149. J. S. Bach—*Well-tempered Clavier, II, Fugue no. 24*

The sixth degree of the minor scale also gives rise to cross relations, since it may be raised when ascending and lowered when either descending or harmonic. In the second of these two examples, showing cross relations involving the submediant, both forms are sounded together, although quite widely spaced.

EX. 150. D. Scarlatti—*Sonata* (Longo ed. no. 379)

EX. 151. D. Scarlatti—*Sonata* (Longo ed. no. 378)

Other cross relations used are of the type seen in example 130, from the Brahms Clarinet Quintet. In the fourth measure the G-natural above is in cross relation with the chromatic cambiata G-sharp following in the lower part.

A bolder kind of cross relation is shown in the next example, between a leading-tone and the seventh of the chord of resolution, in measure two. This is an unusual effect in two-part counterpoint.

EX. 152. J. S. Bach—*Well-tempered Clavier, I, Fugue no. 12*

THE TRITONE

The cross relation of the tritone, where a leading-tone moves to the tonic in the upper voice while the fifth degree descends to the fourth in the lower (called *Diabolus in Musica*), is avoided except when the fourth degree continues its downward movement, as in the following example.

EX. 153. J. S. Bach—*English Suite no. 6, Courante*

THE HARMONIC BASIS

The harmony of the phrase, or melodic unit, should be well organized as to unity and variety as well as to tonality, with or without modulation. The tonal degrees of the scale, tonic, dominant, and subdominant, are the degrees most important to the preservation of a given tonality, and need for that reason to be heard more often than the modal degrees, mediant and submediant, whose function is the decorative one of indicating the mode, whether major or minor. The leading-tone is generally not doubled, as it is a tendency tone. The supertonic might be called a secondary tonal degree, serving as it does so often as dominant of the dominant. While it remains true that the established principles of harmonic doubling of tonal degrees in preference to modal degrees are set aside in favor of significant melodic progression, some care must be exercised lest the continued doubling of inappropriate harmonic factors upset the impression of tonality intended.

If the two melodic lines are fairly flexible and independent rhythmically, the harmonic rhythm may logically show considerable agreement with the metric pulse underlying the music. It is, however, quite possible that the pattern of root movement may be as free of the barlines as the melodic rhythms themselves.

EX. 154. J. S. Bach—*Two-part Invention no. 9*

EXERCISES

In working out exercises it is important to keep in mind the larger aspects and objectives of contrapuntal writing. These may be summarized as follows: (a) the organization of each melodic curve and of the contrapuntal relationship between the curves; (b) the organization of the separate melodic rhythms, with regard to the rhythmic independence of the voices and the balance of rhythmic activity between them; (c) the organization of the harmonic background, especially the coordination of the harmonic rhythm with the melodic rhythm.

Smaller details, such as decisions as to the correctness of a single note, are of much less significance. Moreover, such details vary greatly with the wide diversity of style throughout the period we are studying, while the larger principles indicated above remain valid for counterpoint in any style which embraces harmony as well as melody. The student who has acquired a good knowledge of harmony is urged to write his counterpoint in several different harmonic, melodic, and rhythmic styles.

Additional material for exercises should be selected from musical literature, following the example of the given parts in exercise no. 1. The exercise material in this book cannot be regarded as sufficient practice for those who wish to achieve facility in contrapuntal writing. The questions are intended as specimens of the kind of exercise required, and it is expected that both teacher and student will devise further exercises of a similar nature.

1. Write melodic lines in two-part counterpoint to the parts given below, in accordance with the following schedule. The given parts may be transposed if a change of key or of pitch location is desired.

    (a) A bass in steadily moving notes of equal time value
    (b) An upper part in notes of equal value
    (c) A lower part of comparable importance to the given part
    (d) The same, but an upper part
    (e) A counterpoint having the same pitch location as the given part

In each instance, more than one version should be made.

(from Bach—*Chorale Prelude, Christ lag in Todes Banden*)

(from Beethoven—*Quartet, op. 18, no. 4*)

(from Corelli—*Sonata, op. 3, no. 9*)

(from Bach—*Art of Fugue*)

2. Construct phrases in two-part counterpoint on the following patterns of harmonic rhythm.

(a)

Andante

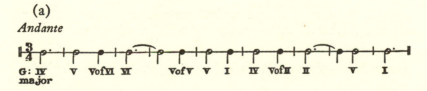

(b)

Moderato

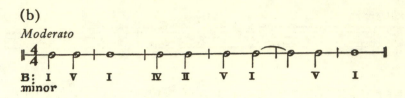

B: I   V   I   IV   II   V   I   V   I
minor

3. Construct a musical sentence of two phrases in two-part counterpoint, fulfilling these specifications:

(a) The first phrase begins in E-flat major and modulates to C minor, ending with a half-cadence in that key.

(b) The second phrase begins in C minor and returns to the original key, ending with an authentic cadence.

4. Construct a phrase in two-part counterpoint in which the element of chromaticism is introduced in both voices.

⇢≫ ≪⇠

CHAPTER SIX

MOTIVE STRUCTURE

I N MOST cases, phrases in instrumental music are made up of smaller
melodic units, called motives. A rigid definition of the limits of a
musical motive is as impractical as a description of the size of a
thought or an idea. Some have called the motive a complete musical
thought, while others have stressed its quality as an irreducible minimum of musical meaning. Here we shall resort to showing by musical
examples the melodic patterns to be designated as motives, many of
which are capable of further subdivision into groups of tones which
we would still call motives. This way of avoiding the direct definition
of the motive permits a degree of flexibility at least, and it has the merit
of being an approach to the subject in terms of music itself.

The length of these motives varies from one beat to three measures,
or even longer. They may contain as few as two notes or as many as
fifteen or more, as will be seen in the examples.

RHYTHMIC TYPES

Most often the motive takes the rhythmic form of an anacrusis,
acting as a long or short up-beat, terminating in a down-beat.

EX. 155. Mozart—*Divertimento for Violin, Viola, and 'Cello, K. 563*

The opposite rhythmic type of motive begins with a down-beat, and ends in an up-beat. This up-beat, it will be noticed, does not serve as an anacrusis leading into the next down-beat. There is a clear impression of punctuation in the line between the motives, like a comma or a slight intake of breath.

EX. 156. Grieg—*Piano Concerto, op. 16*

A third type both begins and ends with a down-beat. The rhythmic effect is positive and block-like, with less feeling of forward motion than in the two other types.

EX. 157. Beethoven—*Quartet, op. 18, no. 1*

The following example by Bach begins with a motive of this third type, and continues with very short motives of the anacrusis type.

EX. 158. J. S. Bach—*Clavier Concerto in D Minor*

Allegro

MELODIES OF ONE MOTIVE

The number of motives used to form a melodic phrase is usually not more than three or four, and often is only one. This indicates a preference of composers for coherence and unity of material, or concentration rather than too much variety of musical thought in one phrase. The melodies in the following three examples are constructed each from a single motive, using principles of motive variation to some extent. In example 159 the motive could be regarded as embracing either three or six notes, as shown by the brackets.

EX. 159. Brahms.—*Intermezzo, op. 117, no. 3*

Andante con moto

EX. 160. Haydn—*Quartet, op. 17, no. 5*

Presto

EX. 161. Schubert—*Sonata, op. 53*

Sometimes development of the line is carried on through the use of only part of the motive. This method is illustrated by the two examples below. In the Haydn melody the motive is of a rhythmic type similar to that in example 156, and the second half of the motive, with slight variations in interval, is employed to extend the phrase. In the Brahms example the motive is first shortened by dropping its first three notes, then by cutting short the terminating down-beat.

EX. 162. Haydn—*Quartet, op. 77, no. 1*

EX. 163. Brahms—*Quartet, op. 51, no. 1*

MOTIVE VARIATION

Motives undergo extensive variation without losing their identity, thus providing considerable variety within the unity of repetition. The most natural variation is that of transposition, which brings not only change in pitch but also some changes in the intervals, due to the new position in the scale.

EX. 164. J. S. Bach—*Organ Trio in G*

EX. 165. Beethoven—*String Trio, op. 9, no. 1*

A motive may be varied by diminution. In the following example, the motive of three notes is first transposed and the time values are halved. On its third appearance, still in diminution, it is extended by the addition of two eighth-notes. The motive marked *b* could be interpreted as a variant of *a*, by contrary motion.

EX. 166. J. S. Bach—*Well-tempered Clavier, I, Fugue no. 14*

Variation by augmentation, the time values doubled, quite naturally has the effect of slowing down the motion of the melody. In this fragment from the Brahms G major violin sonata it is used to mark the return of the theme of the rondo, much as an actual *ritardando* might be applied.

EX. 167. Brahms—*Sonata for Violin and Piano, op. 78*

Inversion, with the intervals of the motive arranged in contrary motion to the original, and retrograde motion (the motive written backwards), are other resources of variation. Retrograde forms are rarely employed since it is very difficult for the ear to recognize a motive played in this fashion. The motive is presented in inversion in the example below.

EX. 168. J. S. Bach—*Two-part Invention no. 1*

Transposition, inversion, and retrograde motion sometimes mean variation so slight as to be hardly noticed. In the following example, the small motive of four sixteenth-notes is an element of unity presented in various forms. A larger classification into motives of three and four beats is indicated by the brackets above the staff. These relationships are to be remarked: *b* is the retrograde inversion of *a; d* is retrograde of *c,* transposed; *f* is either retrograde or inversion of *e,* transposed; *e* is a variant of *a* in one interval, also transposed.

EX. 169. Vivaldi—*Violin Concerto, op. 3, no. 6*

In the process of variation more radical changes may be made in the intervals or the rhythm of the motive. Much the commonest method is to vary the intervals while preserving the rhythmic pattern. In fact, the identity of a motive can in most cases be maintained effectively by the rhythm alone, even when the intervals and the direction of the melodic outline have been completely altered. Compare the forms of the motive in the example below.

EX. 170. Brahms—*Quintet, op. 111*

When there are variations in rhythm as well as in intervals, the derivation of the motive may no longer be evident. The rhythm should be but slightly varied if the thematic connection between the motive and its variant is to be kept, as in example 171. Here the second measure remains recognizable as a variation of the first measure, in spite of a rhythmic alteration which, although slight in appearance, completely upsets the distribution of rhythmic weight in the motive. The third eighth-note, a simple passing-tone, becomes in measure two the tone of chief rhythmic stress, by virtue of its comparative length and its introduction by skip of a fourth.

EX. 171. J. S. Bach—*Two-part Invention no. 5*

Decorative tones of all types may be used to vary the motive. In the following example the outline of the motive is preserved by the tones sounded on the beats. The added notes are factors of the harmony. This is the simplest and most easily followed decorative variation of a motive. Example 173 shows the decorative variation carried a little further, particularly in the new version of motive *a* presented in the third measure.

EX. 172. Brahms—*Symphony no. 4*

EX. 173. Mozart—*Rondo, K. 494*

Finally, the process of variation may result in the formation of a new motive. This is a true function of development in music and, although not strictly within the scope of a study of counterpoint, the principle may appropriately be brought to the student's attention as an aspect of motive variation. In the example below can be seen the progressive change of the motive through three variations. The first variant lacks only one note of the original. The second can still be identified as a variation. The last would certainly not be recognized as the same motive if we had not witnessed the intervening stages of the metamorphosis.

EX. 174. Brahms—*Sextet, op. 18*

See also example 166 for a similar process of evolution in motive structure.

MELODIES OF TWO MOTIVES

When the melody contains two different motives, this circumstance alone may furnish sufficient variety so that little variation of the motives is needed in the course of the phrase. The order of presentation of the two motives is also a source of variety. In the following example, the symmetry of regular alternation of the motives, *a b a b*, is further emphasized by the motives being of equal two measure lengths. Slight variation other than that of transposition is applied to the motives.

EX. 175. Haydn—*Symphony in D Major, no. 101 "Clock"*

Of more interest is the arrangement below, *a a b b a a*. Moreover, the difference in length of the motives *a* and *b* helps to avoid the regularity and sing-song effect felt in example 175.

EX. 176. J. S. Bach—*Well-tempered Clavier, I, Fugue no. 15*

In example 177 the order of motives is *a b b a*, and they are joined in an exceptionally smooth and flowing melodic curve.

EX. 177. Schumann—*Quartet, op. 41, no. 2*

MELODIES OF MORE THAN TWO MOTIVES

Phrases made of three and four motives do not possess the thematic unity of the preceding types, although it is generally possible to interpret some of the motives as variations of others, *e. g.* motive *d* in example 178, which might conceivably have been derived from *b*. Such questions of derivation cannot as a rule be answered with certainty, but arguing the case is always beneficial and stimulating to the musical imagination.

It is logical for certain types of themes, such as rather long fugue subjects, to present several motives as material for subsequent development.

EX. 178. J. S. Bach—*Well-tempered Clavier, II, Fugue no. 13*

ABSENCE OF MOTIVE STRUCTURE

Not all melodies are formed by the procedures just described, nor is motive structure an indispensable attribute of good melody. It will be found extensively in instrumental music as an important element of coherence, but this coherence may be achieved in other ways, and may not at all times be desired by the composer.

One may analyze any melodic line as a long series of different motives, or find grounds for the conclusion that some of these are variants of others. But it would be a mistake to deny that melodies are sometimes developed in complete freedom, without thought of motives and their variation. Such is perhaps the case with the following melody by Beethoven.

EX. 179. Beethoven—*Sonata for Violin and Piano, op. 24*

MOTIVES IN TWO-PART WRITING

When two voices are employed, each part may have its own distinct motive structure, the motives of one voice bearing little or no resemblance to those of the other voice.

EX. 180. Haydn—*Quartet, op. 76, no. 6*

EX. 181. J. S. Bach—*Chromatic Fantasy and Fugue*

The motives need not be of the same length in the two voices. In the example below, the left-hand part consists of one long motive, while the upper part is made up of motives one-fourth as long.

EX. 182. J. S. Bach—*Three-part Invention no. 9*

IMITATION

More commonly, and especially in music of a contrapuntal nature, the same motives will appear in both voices. This is called imitation. The imitation of a motive in another voice may be literal, or it may occur in any of the forms of motive variation described above. Example 183 illustrates the literal imitation, at the fourth above, by the right hand, of the motives in the left-hand part.

EX. 183. Mozart—*Piano Concerto, K. 537*

In the following example, in which the lower voice imitates the upper, the rhythmic pattern of the motives is preserved, while the melodic intervals are changed.

EX. 184. Mozart—*Sonata, K. 330*

With two motives, considerable variety of distribution is possible, with or without motive variation. The motives are not necessarily presented in the same order in both voices.

EX. 185. Handel—*Concerto Grosso no. 10*

Literal imitation of the first motive by the second voice gives the impression that the second voice is to be developed in canon, but in most cases the regular imitation is not carried out beyond a few measures. In the next example the canon at the fourth below is abandoned after three measures. This effect of partial canon was very popular with eighteenth-century composers.

EX. 186. Mozart—*Quartet, K. 575*

The following incomplete canon at the second above is maintained somewhat longer. The two voices involved have about the same pitch location.

EX. 187. Handel—*Sonata for Two Oboes with Figured Bass, no. 6*

Occasionally the second voice imitates the first by contrary motion, creating a type of melodic inversion.

EX. 188. J. S. Bach—*Chorale Prelude, Wenn wir in höchsten Nöten sein*

The imitation often begins in the second voice before the original motive has finished, causing an overlapping of motives. This happens in many of the examples given in this chapter and may be said to be a characteristic feature of contrapuntal style.

EX. 189. Mozart—*Sonata for Violin and Piano, K. 402*

SEQUENCE

The sequence, by definition, involves both imitation and motive structure. By repetition of a melodic pattern transposed, the melodic line imitates itself, as in the following example. Here there are two motives, one for each part.

EX. 190. Haydn—*Symphony in G Major, "Surprise" no. 94*

Imitation of motives between the two voices gives added interest to harmonic sequences. In the next example a simple root progression by descending steps is by this means transformed into a fairly complex contrapuntal texture. Especially noteworthy are the cross accents of the melodic rhythms, and their relation to the rhythm of the harmonic changes.

EX. 191. J. S. Bach—*Italian Concerto*

When two motives are used in the sequence, the imitation may alternate between the voices, giving a motive structure of *a b a* for one voice, against *b a b* for the other, as in the following.

EX. 192. J. S. Bach—*Organ Fugue in C Minor*

EXERCISES

1. Apply the following procedures of variation to the above motive: (a) transposition, (b) diminution, (c) inversion, (d) retrograde motion, (e) variation of intervals, not rhythm, (f) variation of rhythm, not intervals, (g) variation of both rhythm and intervals, (h) addition of decorative tones.

2. Construct three different melodic phrases (single line), using exclusively the following motive.

3. Construct three different melodic phrases using in each the following two motives exclusively.

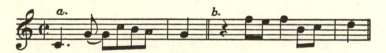

4. Construct a phrase in two-part counterpoint, using only the two motives below, and employing imitation.

5. On the harmonic patterns given, write sequences in two-part counterpoint, with imitation.

(a)

(b)

(c)

6. To the following given parts, add second parts in two-part counterpoint, using imitation.

Allegro

(a)

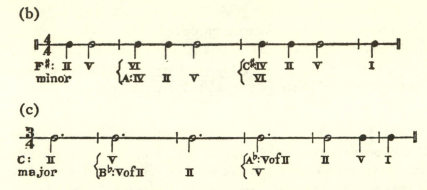

(from Bach—*The Musical Offering*)

Allegro moderato

(b)

(from Mozart—*Sonata for Violin and Piano, K. 402*)

7. Write two separate phrases in two-part counterpoint, using only two motives. In the first phrase, each voice is made from one motive and there is no imitation between the voices. In the second phrase, constructed from the same motives, both motives are used in both voices. The phrases should be ten or twelve measures in length.

CHAPTER SEVEN

THREE-PART COUNTERPOINT

THE texture of three-part writing has always recommended itself to composers by virtue of the contrapuntal clarity it retains, while at the same time affording an adequate degree of harmonic fullness. A great contrapuntal era, the Baroque, centered its polyphonic structures around a basic three-part construction (the triosonata, organ works for two manuals and pedal, etc.). It is significant that in most of the four-voiced fugues of Bach a large proportion of the counterpoint is in three parts, the complete texture of four voices being used for variety and climax. Three-part writing is especially effective for keyboard music. Also, many a page of orchestral score, when octave doublings and subordinate harmonic background notes have been accounted for, will prove to rest upon a fundamental basis of three "real" parts.

Just as in two-part counterpoint, the voices, compared with one another, are not always of equal melodic importance. Subordinate voices may be simple counterpoints moving in notes of unchanging time value, such as eighths or sixteenths. The absence of rhythmic interest in the subordinate parts helps to preserve their function as accompanying voices and gives added prominence in the texture to the principal voice. These parts may nevertheless possess considerable interest as melodic lines and, as in example 193, often do much more than fill out the harmony.

EX. 193. J. S. Bach—*Chorale Prelude, Nun freut euch*

This predominance of one voice over the other two can be brought about by other means. For instance, in example no. 210 the orchestration gives prominence to the upper voice, although the two lower parts would seem to have more rhythmic interest. The combination of violas and 'celli far overbalances the single bassoon and the low basses.

More often there is but one part moving in equal values as a foil for the two-part rhythmically varied counterpoint in the other voices.

EX. 194. J. S. Bach—*Three-part Invention no. 1*

EX. 195. Handel—*Concerto Grosso no. 5*

EX. 196. Beethoven—*Sonata for Violin and Piano, op. 30, no 1*

If two of the parts move in parallel thirds or sixths they become practically one part, so that what appears to be a three-part texture is actually more like two-part writing. In example 197 the lowest voice
possesses little rhythmic independence but it has at least the contrast of

EX. 197. Haydn—*Quartet, op. 77, no. 1*

melodic curve. Example 198 is unusual in that the parallel thirds occur
between outside voices. In the third of these examples, no. 199, the
parallel motion is just as continually present but in changing pairs of
voices, so that there is more independence in the three individual
melodic lines.

While examples 197, 198 and 199 show that three-part counterpoint
in practical use varies a great deal in respect to the relative significance
of the three lines, the higher and more satisfactory type of three-part

EX. 198. Mendelssohn—*Organ Sonata, op. 65, no. 2*

Allegro moderato

EX. 199. Handel—*Suite no. 3, Courante*

counterpoint consists of a combination of three melodies which are fairly independent in their rhythmic patterns and melodic curves. They have the same harmonic basis and agree in general style, and their motive structure will usually show some imitation between the voices. Following are four examples in different styles.

EX. 200. J. S. Bach—*The Art of Fugue, Contrapunctus I*

EX. 201. Beethoven—*Sonata for 'Cello and Piano, op. 102, no. 1*

EX. 202. Franck—*Quartet*

EX. 203. Mozart—*Quartet, K. 387*

The addition of a third voice brings very little in the way of modification of the principles underlying two-part writing. Considered by pairs, the voices bear the same relationships as in two-part counterpoint. The interval of a perfect fourth, however, is no longer regarded as a dissonant interval unless its lower tone is at the same time the lowest of the three voices. The presence of a third or fifth beneath seems to stabilize this interval.

In general, what takes place in the outside (upper and lower) voices is much more prominent to the ear than activities involving the inner voice. Direct octaves and fifths, and approaches to dissonant intervals by similar motion, are less pronounced when one of the parts is an inside part. The acceptability of these effects must nevertheless still be judged according to the merits of each case, on the basis of rhythmic accentuation of the interval in question and the desired independence of the voices.

The progression of a diminished fifth to a perfect fifth, usually avoided in two-part writing, is commonly used in two upper voices when the bass moves to the third of the chord represented by the second interval.

EX. 204

EX. 205. J. S. Bach—*Organ Fugue in E Minor*

The cross relation of the tritone is freely used when the progression from fifth to fourth degree takes place in the inner part.

EX. 206. J. S. Bach—*Organ Fugue in A Major*

EX. 207. J. S. Bach—*Well-tempered Clavier, I, Prelude no. 23*

HARMONY

As will be seen from almost any of the examples, harmonic principles of doubling are constantly ignored in favor of effective melodic movement. On the other hand, doublings of modal degrees are not allowed to become so marked as to weaken the total effect of tonality, and doublings of tendency tones are carefully managed so that independence of the voices will not be seriously impaired.

Although three parts are now available, it is not necessary to include all the factors of the chords. The fifth is often omitted, permitting doubling of the root or the third. Even the third is sometimes left out, and fifth and third, without root, are used on occasion to represent the complete triad.

Harmonic dissonances are employed but if the style is at all contrapuntal the dissonant factors are ordinarily capable of being analyzed as contrapuntal tones. In the following example, recognition of the sequence of seventh chords as such seems preferable to complex explanations based on delayed resolutions of the suspensions, etc.

EX. 208. Haydn—*Oxford Symphony*

In example 209 there is less emphasis on harmony. Two analyses of the harmonic progressions are offered. The lower, with a chord on each beat, is certainly heard, but the upper and simpler line of symbols gives an entirely satisfactory explanation of the harmonic background upon which the voices are constructed.

EX. 209. J. S. Bach—*Well-tempered Clavier, II, Prelude no. 9*

In the next example note the following harmonic features: *a* tonic six-four chord; *b* dominant seventh chord with seventh in the bass; *c* submediant seventh chord; *d* doubled third degree; *e* weak root progression II–IV.

EX. 210. Beethoven—*Symphony no. 9*

Melodic chromaticism is most successful when sparingly employed, and combined with diatonic movement in other voices.

EX. 211. Beethoven—*Sonata for Violin and Piano, op. 96*

VERTICAL SONORITIES

An important aspect of all counterpoint is the effect in sound of combinations of intervals resulting from the meeting of independent voices.

EX. 212. Handel—*Suite no. 1, Allemande*

In this example, the following superpositions of intervals are found at the points indicated:

    a perfect fifth on minor seventh
    b minor seventh on perfect fifth
    c major seventh on minor third
    d minor seventh on major sixth
    e minor seventh on minor sixth

In example 213
    a perfect fourth on major seventh
    b perfect fourth on perfect octave

In example 214:
    a major ninth on minor ninth
    b minor ninth on major ninth
    c major ninth on major ninth

EX. 213. J. S. Bach—*French Suite no. 1, Allemande*

EX. 214. J. S. Bach—*Partita no. 5, Gigue*

G: IV   V   I   VI   II   V   I

It is true that these combinations of notes can be related to series of thirds, identified as known chords. Thus example 212, *a* and *b*, would suggest a dominant eleventh chord; 213, *a*, a seventh chord on the submediant; and 214, *b*, a supertonic ninth. But these are artificial designations and we know that the dissonant tones are sounding against much simpler chords.

The student is urged to read over as much contrapuntal music as possible, noting these combinations, or vertical cross sections. They not only are characteristic signs of good counterpoint, but also they represent an evolutionary stage in the establishment of new chords. The particular order of superposition of the intervals and the resultant spacing give each of these combinations an individuality much appreciated by composers in the twentieth century.

HARMONIC ACTIVITY

The frequency with which root changes occur is subject to all variations in this as in all types of counterpoint. It is perhaps possible to say that the fewer chords in the phrase, the more contrapuntal the music, but contrapuntal music can nevertheless possess a great deal of harmonic activity. In the following example a change of root is made on nearly every eighth-note in a fast tempo. The contrapuntal quality of the music is due to the linear independence of accent and melodic curve.

EX. 215. Mozart—*Eine kleine Gigue, K. 574*

A comparison of the two illustrations below will show that harmonic dissonance is not in itself capable of imparting contrapuntal feeling to the texture, and that the contrapuntal quality can be present along with active harmony. In both excerpts a root change is felt on each successive eighth-note, or nearly so. The Bach example is much less dissonant harmonically than that by Haydn yet it is unquestionably the more contrapuntal of the two.

EX. 216. Haydn—*Sonata no. 16*

EX. 217. J. S. Bach—*Well-tempered Clavier, II, Fugue no. 5*

SPACING

Spacing of the three parts is to a large extent influenced by the pitch location of the parts involved, and this is in turn determined by the choice of instruments. When freedom is permitted by these factors, the spacing will still be affected by the direction of the melodic curves.

Spacing of all kinds is used in contrapuntal texture, the placing of the sonorities being more a matter of taste and style than of any observable rule. On a keyboard instrument it is natural to depart from an even distribution by placing the two upper voices close together within the reach of the right hand, leaving a wider space between them and the third voice. This procedure is also followed occasionally in writing for other than keyboard instruments, although as already remarked, the instruments employed will be the chief deciding factor.

EX. 218. Schumann—*Organ Fugue on the Name of Bach, op. 60, no. 1*

EX. 219. C. P. E. Bach—*Trio in G Major*

The opposite method, placing the two lower voices close, with the wider spaces between the upper two parts, is not usually to be recommended. The sound of the pair of voices in close position in a low register lacks clarity and is less agreeable to the ear, but such an arrangement is sometimes used for variety.

EX. 220. J. S. Bach—*Well-tempered Clavier, I, Fugue no. 20*

When a keyboard instrument is combined with a string or wind instrument the composer considers the sonority of each as an individual, as well as the sound of both together. The student is advised to give some thought to this point in his perusal of music in connection with contrapuntal studies, but he is also reminded that mastery of idiomatic writing for instruments demands special study of the instruments themselves, a subject rather beyond the scope of a study of counterpoint.

An example is given here to illustrate the effectiveness of an unusually wide spacing of three lines for violin and piano.

EX. 221. Brahms—*Sonata for Violin and Piano, op. 78*

Vivace ma non troppo

As a rule the spacing is continually changing, combining the above arrangements with a disposition in which the parts are more evenly spaced, in close or open position.

EX. 222. Beethoven—*Quartet, op. 131*

When all three voices are of the same pitch location the parts will inevitably cross over one another (examples 223, 224).

EX. 223. J. S. Bach—*Brandenburg Concerto no. 4*

In both of these examples by Bach the part in running eighth-notes acts as accompanying counterpoint to the other two voices, which are in each instance unified by the imitation of motives. The grouping of two and one is further accentuated by the different tone colors employed, one violin against two flutes, and one flute against two violin parts. Note the diversity in rhythmic value of the notes sounding together in any given measure, a diversity not only in the lengths of the notes but also in their rhythmic stress.

The student is referred to examples 226, and 227 for further illustration of this point.

EX. 224. J. S. Bach—*Suite no. 2, Rondeau*

Unisons are employed in the manner described in the chapter dealing with two-part counterpoint (see page 81). As in the last two examples, an occasional unison will occur when two or more voices have similar pitch locations and so may cross each other rather frequently. This crossing of voices is more and more to be expected as the number of voices increases, unless the melodic curves are to move in very restricted range. In three-part counterpoint unisons are rare between the upper and lower voices, although it is possible to have all three parts in unison, as in example 225. Here the branching out of the voices from a common tone is a typical contrapuntal effect.

EX. 225. Mozart—*Quartet, K. 575*

In contrapuntal style the voices do not usually start their phrases at the same moment, especially if important motives are being imitated at the beginning of the phrase. Likewise the voices will drop out at different points in the course of the music, except that they are likely to finish together at cadences. This entering and leaving at different times contributes to the independence of the parts and adds variety to the texture.

The entrance of a significant motive following a short silence is also a means of calling the listener's attention to a different voice, like the second oboe part in the third measure of example 226.

EX. 226. J. S. Bach—*Suite in C Major, Ouverture*

The introduction of rests of short duration into the melodic lines lightens the texture and helps to clarify the motive structure. Rests can be employed without destroying the continuity of the melodic lines, as may be seen from the following example.

EX. 227. J. S. Bach—*Three-part Invention no. 9*

EXERCISES

In writing exercises in three-part counterpoint, the main points to be kept in mind are: the individual quality of the melodic lines; the relative independence of the melodic curves and rhythms; the balance of rhythmic activity; the organization of the harmony and of the harmonic rhythm; motive structure and imitation; spacing; and the vertical combinations of intervals created by the counterpoint.

The student is advised to cultivate an attitude which we may call "contrapuntal curiosity." By this we mean the urge to seek combinations of tones which give sonorities new to him, but which he can nevertheless justify through logic and principles of musical practice, in other words to make some discoveries of his own in the realm of contrapuntal possibilities. Excesses in this direction on the student's part are excusable as representing a phase in his development and as a natural result of concentration on the contrapuntal element in music.

1. (a) On each of the three harmonic patterns given below, write two different phrases in three-part counterpoint in which one of the voices moves in steady eighth-notes, while the other two are varied in rhythm.

(b) On each of the three patterns construct two different phrases in three-part counterpoint, one voice in steady eighth-notes, one voice in steady sixteenths, and the third voice in varied rhythm.

(c) On each of the three patterns construct three different phrases in three-part counterpoint, all the voices being of equal importance melodically, and using imitation.

(a)

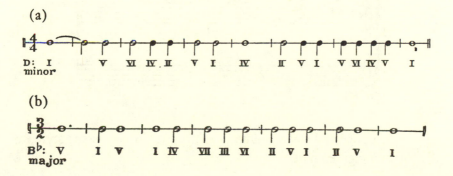

(b)

(c)

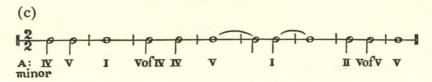

2. Continue, for one phrase in each case, the following beginnings. Maintain unity of style and employ imitation based on the motives suggested by the given fragments.

(a) *Andante* (Bach)   (b) *Allegro* (Mozart)

(c) *Moderato* (Schumann)

3. Add upper and lower contrapuntal parts, in consistent style, to the following given part.

(from Bach—*Organ Fugue in E Minor*)

4. Add a suitable inner part to the following.

(from Handel—*Sonata for Flute with Figured Bass*)

5. Construct a musical sentence of three phrases in three-part counterpoint, according to the following specifications:

    (a) The instruments used are violin, viola, and violoncello.

    (b) The first phrase is in G major, ending with a half cadence.

    (c) The second phrase modulates to E minor, ending with a cadence in that key.

    (d) The third phrase returns to the original key.

6. Construct a musical sentence of three phrases in three-part counterpoint, according to the following specifications:

(a) The instruments used are flute, oboe, and clarinet.

(b) The first phrase is in A minor, ending with a deceptive cadence.

(c) The second phrase contains a modulating sequence, ending in a key other than A.

(d) The third phrase returns to the original key.

꘏꘏꘏ ꘏꘏꘏

COUNTERPOINT IN MORE
THAN THREE PARTS

WHEN the number of contrapuntal voices is greater than three, one very natural result is a fullness of harmony not felt in two- and three-part writing. This is especially a character-istic of four-part counterpoint, since the four-voiced texture is by far the commonest basis of harmonic music. The parts usually stand in the broad relationship of soprano, alto, tenor, and bass, and tend to combine vertically into triads with one factor doubled, or into com-plete seventh chords.

Contrapuntally, this tendency is a defect rather than a virtue. In four-part writing the problem of achieving independence of the me-lodic lines is rendered more difficult by the fact that we hear almost any combination of four notes as a chord. The combinations we accept and classify as chords originated in this way.

The student who has learned about chords and chord progressions in the study of harmony will ask what is the difference between four-part harmony and four-part counterpoint. These are not, however, mutually exclusive concepts. All four-part counterpoint is harmonic because the combination of four tones makes a chord. Four-part har-mony, on the other hand, is contrapuntal only to the degree that the four parts have individuality and independence as melodic lines, accord-ing to the principles we have discussed in previous chapters.

It would not be easy to say whether the following excerpt should be designated as harmonic or as contrapuntal. Considered sep-arately each voice is fairly melodic. But the parts are lacking in inde-pendence of rhythm and there is little independence in the combined melodic curves.

EX. 228. Beethoven—*Quartet, op. 18, no. 5*

The next example is much more contrapuntal in that each line possesses an individual rhythmic vigor and the melodic curves are more independent than in the Beethoven phrase. There is strong emphasis on the harmonic effect, however, as all parts come together to complete the harmony on all beats.

EX. 229. Handel—*Concerto Grosso no. 1*

Greater independence of melodic rhythm and curve, as shown in example 230, adds to the contrapuntal as opposed to the harmonic effect. Note that the high points of the curves occur at different times, and that at least one of the vertical combinations of intervals, such as that on the first beat of measure two, does not form one of the chords in common use. In comparison with example 228, this excerpt goes far toward demonstrating the difference between four-part harmony and four-part counterpoint.

EX. 230. J. S. Bach—*The Art of Fugue, Contrapunctus IV*

Observations regarding harmonic doubling made in connection with two- and three-part counterpoint remain valid for counterpoint in more than three parts. The primary concern is for the formation of good melodic lines, but the tonality should not be weakened by excessive doubling of the modal degrees.

With more than three parts many more variations in the relative importance of the voices become possible. Very often an inside part, or perhaps the bass, may be markedly subordinate in character, and lacking in melodic significance. Voices written in notes of equal time values serve as background or decoration to the more important, rhythmically organized, voices. In the following illustration may be seen two such parts, the bass in eighths and the tenor in sixteenths.

EX. 231. J. S. Bach—*Chorale Prelude, Es ist das Heil*

The lesser importance of parts of this type probably accounts for the fact that they are sometimes permitted to make certain consecutive octaves and other faulty motion against more important voices, a procedure which would be avoided between two voices of equal melodic and thematic significance. Note the octaves in this passage.

EX. 232. Beethoven—*Symphony no. 3*

Decisions as to the acceptability of direct octaves and fifths and approaches to dissonant intervals by similar motion, are made on the basis of the amount of emphasis given the intervals in question. If the voices involved are inside voices much less emphasis and prominence is felt, and some progressions are then used which would be less acceptable between outside parts.

The striking series of consecutive fifths in the example below cannot be dismissed with a remark that the voices concerned are unimportant. It is true that they are inside parts but they are not subordinate voices. The fifths receive prominence since they occur as resolutions of preceding dissonances and the spacing brings them to the listener's attention. Although this is certainly an unusual passage the progressions may be related to harmonic practice through the circumstance that the bass moves to the third of the chord on the second beat of each measure. (*See* example 204 in Chapter Seven.)

EX. 233. Haydn—*Quartet, op. 17, no. 6*

A different aspect of relationship between the four voices is illustrated in example 234. Here is shown the entrance in the top voice of the well-known passacaglia theme, at the start of the thirteenth variation. Obviously this is the most important voice, but it is worthy of notice that the other three parts are significant contrapuntal voices, anything but subordinate, with strong rhythmic structure, and demanding attention through the imitation of well-defined motives. This is four-part counterpoint of a high level.

EX. 234. J. S. Bach—*Passacaglia for Organ*

The process of doubling one part by another in thirds or sixths may be applied to the voices in pairs, so that a four-voiced texture is reduced to two fundamental lines with harmonic doubling or thickening. It is a way of gaining a full sonority without complicating the rhythmic texture but does not, of course, create four-part counterpoint.

Of the two examples below, that by Mozart is the more interesting for the vertical sonorities produced. If the thickening of the two melodic lines were intensified by the addition of other intervals to each part, one would have an example of so-called "chord streams," used by certain twentieth-century composers.

In the fragment from the Mendelssohn quartet it will be noticed that the two outside voices are paired against the two inner parts.

EX. 235. Mozart—*Sonata, K. 533*

EX. 236. Mendelssohn—*Quartet, op. 80*

Allegro vivace assai

In the following example by Mozart, what appears to be four-part counterpoint is discovered on hearing to be a three-voiced texture. The parts for piano and 'cello are two versions of the same part.

EX. 237. Mozart—*Piano Quartet, K. 478*

Andante

SPACING

Four-part writing gives much opportunity for variety in spacing, from the very wide disposition shown in example 238 to the close position of example 239. The intervals between the voices are, of course, always changing with the movements of the melodic curves.

EX. 238. Beethoven—*Quartet, op. 127*

EX. 239. J. S. Bach—*Toccata con Fuga no. 2*

The three upper voices may be placed in close position, leaving a wide space between them and the bass, an arrangement especially adaptable to the keyboard.

EX. 240. J. S. Bach—*Well-tempered Clavier, I, Fugue no. 4*

It is likewise fairly common for the widest space to be found between the inside parts, dividing the texture into two pairs of voices, as in the example below.

EX. 241. J. S. Bach—*The Art of Fugue, Contrapunctus I*

VERTICAL SONORITIES

The vertical cross sections of four-part counterpoint give sonorities which are in some ways less suggestive than the open effects of three-part writing, but they are often more dissonant. Dissonance is an essential element in counterpoint since it arises from disagreement. It also contributes movement through its tendency forwards toward resolution. The problem is one of retaining coherence of harmony while obtaining the most in contrapuntal effect by means of dissonances. The harmony is sometimes obscured or uncertain momentarily, as in the first half of the second measure in the example following.

EX. 242. J. S. Bach—*Well-tempered Clavier, I, Fugue no. 24*

Here the three upper parts quite evidently suggest harmony foreign to the bass tone D. Without the bass, the first two beats of measure two would be heard as supertonic followed by dominant harmony. The D, coming after the preceding dominant chord, implies the tonic harmony to which the other parts finally agree on the third beat. The effect is slightly more complex than the comparatively common suspension of dominant harmony over the tonic, as in the third measure (with modulation to F-sharp).

Regarded by interval vertically, the first half of measure two makes an eleventh chord on the mediant.

In example 243, consider the following vertical relationships:

a a combination of intervals that might be called a dominant thirteenth chord, also motion in parallel ninths between the outside voices, violin and bass

b parallel seconds, oboe and violin; meeting of three voices in the minor second, F, E

c crossing of the three upper voices

d the appoggiatura G-natural in the flute against the oboe's G-sharp

e momentary effect of a chord of fourths, B, E, A, D

f prominent movement of diminished to perfect fifth in oboe and violin

g open fifth and fourth sonority just before the final chord

EX. 243. J. S. Bach—*Brandenburg Concerto no. 2*

IMITATION

As in all types of counterpoint, imitation is freely used. It may serve as a unifying element in the individual lines (example 244), or the motives may be passed about in all the parts (example 245). In the latter example, notice that the motive presented in the tenor appears in augmentation in the bass, and in inversion in the soprano.

The element of imitation may be present as a natural consequence of writing as many as four parts in consistent style. In fact, experience shows that it is not easy to compose a phrase in four-part counterpoint with no imitation at all. This unconscious imitation, resulting from a unity of melodic style, may be seen in examples 241 and 243. Although in these examples one can find similarities between motives, the difference between this coherence and the deliberate exploitation of imitation in motive structure is at once apparent upon comparison with the following excerpts.

EX. 244. Mozart—*Quartet, K. 387*

EX. 245. J. S. Bach—*Organ Fugue in C Major*

The imitation need not, of course, occur in all the voices, as examination of the illustrations given will show. In example 242, the only significant motive, that in sixteenth-notes, appears alternately in the lower and upper parts. In the Schumann example following, the three lower parts are in imitation and are by this means set apart as accompaniment to the melody in the first violin.

EX. 246. Schumann—*Quartet, op. 41, no. 2*

Another arrangement, often met with in fugal episodes, is that in which the voices imitate in pairs. Any of the possible combinations may be used: bass with tenor, alto with soprano; bass with alto, tenor with soprano; bass with soprano, tenor with alto. The first of these dispositions is shown in the example below.

EX. 247. J. S. Bach—*Clavier Concerto in D Minor*

In the next illustration, the viola imitates the first violin by contrary motion. The second violin is imitated by the 'cello in similar motion at the fifth below. This fragment is an excellent instance of transparency in texture resulting from the placing of the instrumental voices and the use of rests. Examination of the entire development section of this movement is recommended.

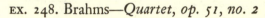

EX. 248. Brahms—*Quartet, op. 51, no. 2*

Example 249, a brilliant passage from a fast quartet movement, shows close imitation between the two violins, while viola and 'cello develop independent motives. The melodic curves possess real contrapuntal sweep.

In the first six measures the two violin parts show a way of making counterpoint out of a simple scale in thirds. Taking the two parts together, the upper notes form a scale of A minor, starting on E. The eighth-notes form the parallel thirds below. By the device of exchanging instruments on alternate beats and introducing the short suspensions an effective two-part contrapuntal formula is created. Also to be noted is the extraordinarily wide spacing between the 'cello part and the upper voices.

EX. 249. Haydn—*Quartet, op. 65, no. 5*

Four-part counterpoint should find its ideal application in string quartet writing, where individuality of the four instrumental parts is highly desirable. Perusal of the vast string quartet literature shows, however, that the composer does not always find it appropriate for his expressive purposes, and that the four-part contrapuntal texture proves the more effective when not continually employed.

FIVE-PART COUNTERPOINT

Counterpoint in more than four parts is uncommon. More often than not, a five- or six-voiced texture will prove to contain at least one part so deficient in melodic interest that it cannot be called a real contrapuntal voice. The texture tends to thickness and obscurity of the individual parts, and unless it is very skillfully managed the effect produced is rather one of harmony than of weaving voices.

Writing in five and six parts is excellent contrapuntal practice. The student will discover that after working in these textures for a time he will feel more freedom and flexibility in three- and four-part writing.

Examples 250 through 255 are to be studied with special attention to these points:

(a) Spacing—its effect on the clarity of the texture.

EX. 250. J. S. Bach—*Brandenburg Concerto no. 4*

(b) The use of rests to lighten the texture and permit entries of motives to be heard.

(c) Melodic activity—whether the voices are all active at the same time, and the effect of this on the clarity of the music.

(d) Imitation—its value in calling attention to the separate voices in turn, and as a unifying element.

(e) Doubling of harmonic factors.

(f) Vertical sonorities on important beats.

(g) Harmonic rhythm.

The student is urged to consult in their entirety the works from which these examples are taken, noticing especially the proportionate amount of five or six-part texture in a whole movement, and its relative effectiveness as compared with the rest of the music. Finding other examples in other works, including those of the twentieth century, will also help him to form a true conception of the place of complex counterpoint in musical composition.

EX. 251. Mozart—*Symphony, K. 551*

EX. 252. J. S. Bach—*Well-tempered Clavier, I, Fugue no. 22*

EX. 253. Mozart—*String Quintet, K. 593*

Allegro

SIX-PART COUNTERPOINT

EX. 254. J. S. Bach—*Chorale Prelude, Aus tiefer Not*

EX. 255. J. S. Bach—*The Musical Offering, Ricercare a 6*

For purposes of study it has been thought advisable to adopt the phrase, or melodic unit, as the basis for the form of all exercises. The reader should be reminded, however, that in actual practice the texture of music is ever changing. The same phrase may be partly harmonic and partly contrapuntal. The composer may elect to vary the contrapuntal texture in the course of the phrase anywhere from two to five or six voices, and he may also vary the contrapuntal quality of the part writing for reasons of taste and expression. The student will derive much benefit from a close study of this practical application in the works of different masters. But in the exercises he will be wise to insist on carrying out through at least a whole phrase whatever kind of contrapuntal problem he sets out to solve.

Some may wish to try their hand at counterpoint in seven and eight parts. In this it is important to keep to the standards of good counterpoint and refuse to accept solutions which have any parts that lack a reasonable degree of melodic value. If this principle is not adhered to, such writing is useless as technical study.

EXERCISES

1. (a) On each of the three harmonic patterns given below, write two different phrases in four-part counterpoint in which one voice moves in steady eighth-notes, one voice in steady sixteenth-notes, and the other two voices in varied rhythm.

(b) On each of the three patterns construct two different phrases in four-part counterpoint, one voice being a predominant melodic line, with the three accompanying voices in imitation among themselves.

(c) On each of the three patterns construct two different phrases in four-part counterpoint, with imitation among all four voices.

(a)

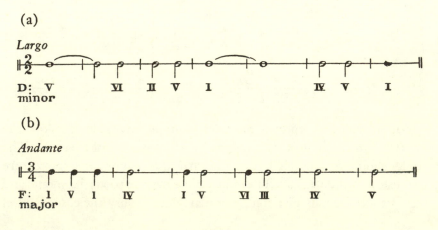

Largo

D: V minor   VI   II   V   I   IV   V   I

(b)

Andante

F: I   V   I   IV   I   V   VI   III   IV   V
major

(c)

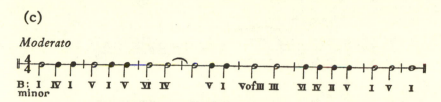

Moderato

B: I IV I V I V VI IV V I VofIII III VI IV II V I V I
minor

2. Continue, for one phrase in each case, the following beginnings.

Moderato (Bach)

(a)

Allegretto (Mozart)

(b)

(c)

3. Add three contrapuntal parts to the following given parts. Several different versions should be made, varying the spacing and other textural features, as well as the amount and type of imitation used. Indicate the instruments employed, and vary the instrumental combinations in the different versions. It is permissible to transpose the given parts to other pitch locations and to other keys. The harmony and general style of the added parts must be in keeping with the given parts.

(a)

(from A. Scarlatti—*Fugue in F Minor*)

(b)

(from Bach—*Chorale Prelude, Jesu meine Freude*)

4. Construct a musical sentence of three phrases in four-part counterpoint, according to the following specifications:

   (a) The instruments are two violins, viola, and violoncello.

   (b) The first phrase is in E minor, ending with a deceptive cadence.

   (c) The second phrase is in a different key.

   (d) The third phrase returns to E minor.

5. Construct a musical sentence of three phrases in four-part counterpoint, according to the following specifications:

   (a) The instruments are flute, oboe, clarinet, and bassoon.

   (b) The first phrase begins in C major and modulates to E-flat major.

   (c) The second phrase modulates back to C major and ends with a half cadence.

   (d) The third phrase begins exactly like the first phrase but remains in C major, ending with an authentic cadence.

5a. Construct a similar piece in four-part counterpoint, for organ. Follow the same plan of phrases and modulations, but choose two different keys. Arrange the parts so that two voices may be played with the right hand, one with the left, and the bass on the pedals. In this piece let the texture be closely knit by fairly continuous imitation throughout of one important motive.

6. Add four voices to the following given bass.

Andante

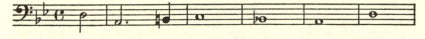

(from Bach—*The Art of Fugue*)

7. Add five voices to the following given bass.

Adagio

(from Bach—*Chorale Variations, Sei gegrüsset*)

CHAPTER NINE

INVERTIBLE COUNTERPOINT

IT IS typical of contrapuntal style that thematic material is handed about, so to speak, in such a way that melodies first heard in upper voices appear later in lower voices, and vice versa. If one wishes to retain the original form of the melodic lines exactly, throughout such transposition, the parts have to be written in invertible counterpoint. The term invertible refers here to the order of the voices, not to the voices themselves. Inversion of the order of the voices, for instance by placing the bass part in the soprano and the soprano part in the bass, is not to be confused with the inversion of melodies, the presentation of melodies in contrary motion, to be discussed in a later chapter.

When two voices are involved the invertible counterpoint is called double counterpoint. The interval of inversion is determined by noting the interval of upward transposition of the lower voice, the upper voice remaining stationary.

EX. 256

It will be seen from the illustration that in the inversion at the octave the lower voice has been transposed up an octave, thus becoming the upper voice. In the inversion at the tenth the lower voice has been transposed up a tenth; in the inversion at the twelfth, up a twelfth; in that at the fifteenth, up a double octave, or fifteenth.

The interval of inversion is less easily ascertained when both voices are transposed. The amount of transposition is equal to the sum of the intervals of transposition in opposite directions of both voices. Shown in the example below are further transpositions of the original pattern in example 256. At *a*, the lower voice has been moved up an octave, and the upper voice down an octave. The interval of inversion is therefore the fifteenth. At *b*, the lower voice has been moved up an octave and the upper voice down a fifth, making the inversion at the twelfth. At *c*, the inversion amounts to a tenth plus an octave, but this extra octave is disregarded in naming the inversion as being at the tenth. In *d*, the inversion is, of course, at the octave, the upper part having been moved instead of the lower.

EX. 257

Double counterpoint may be written at other intervals than those illustrated but, as will be readily appreciated by experiment, the other transpositions are so restricted in possibilities for musical results that their chief value is as technical problems or exercises. In the practice of composers, double counterpoint is almost wholly limited to inversions at the octave, tenth, twelfth, and fifteenth.

DOUBLE COUNTERPOINT AT THE OCTAVE

In inversion at the octave, the following changes take place in the harmonic intervals:

unison becomes octave	fifth becomes fourth
second " seventh	sixth " third
third " sixth	seventh " second
fourth " fifth	octave " unison

From the table it will be observed that the dissonant intervals remain dissonant on inversion. The consonant intervals remain consonant
with the exception of the fifth, which becomes a fourth. Since the
perfect fourth is a dissonant interval in two-part writing, this means
that the fifth must be treated as a dissonant interval so that the counterpoint will be equally good when it is inverted.

As to the method of writing double counterpoint, the system of trial
and error is the most practical. It is best to work out the original and
the inversion at the same time, rather than attempt to complete one
voice before writing the other. One can to a certain extent reason as
well as imagine the effect of the inversion of a given measure, but in
the last analysis the result must be tested by reading or playing the
two parts together.

In double counterpoint at the octave the two voices must at no
time be more than an octave apart, otherwise the octave transposition
will be insufficient to place the lower part above the other. This re-
striction makes it harder to write counterpoint having melodic interest
but this close type of double counterpoint is very useful for keeping
within desired limits of range in a composition like the fugue. Fugue
subject and countersubject are often composed in double counterpoint
at the octave so that they do not together cover too wide a range in
pitch while being at the same time capable of inversion.

EX. 258. J. S. Bach—*The Art of Fugue, Contrapunctus VIII*

From this and from succeeding examples voices have been omitted when they do not have a bearing on the point to be illustrated. Only the two voices taking part in the double counterpoint are given.

To effect the inversion and a change of key as well, the upper voice in example 258 has been transposed down an octave and a fourth. The lower voice has itself been transposed down a fourth, so the situation is as though the lower voice remained stationary while the upper voice moved an octave. The inversion is therefore at the octave.

Below is another example of two-part counterpoint capable of inversion at the octave, although Bach chose to invert it only at the wider interval of the fifteenth.

EX. 259. J. S. Bach—*Well-tempered Clavier, I, Fugue no. 14*

Crossing of the voices should happen very rarely in double counterpoint, since it makes inversion impossible at the point where the crossing occurs, as on the first beat of the second measure in the following example.

EX. 260. Beethoven—*Symphony no. 7*

Inversion

DOUBLE COUNTERPOINT AT THE FIFTEENTH

A total transposition of two octaves gives more freedom of movement for the melodic lines. Double counterpoint at the fifteenth differs from that at the octave only in this matter of range and the general term "at the octave" is often used broadly to mean any number of octaves. Ordinarily, however, the term "at the fifteenth" carries the implication that the counterpoint will not invert at the single octave. The example following shows an inversion at the fifteenth, each voice having been moved an octave. As far as the range is concerned, inversion at the octave would be feasible, but Bach did not use this, possibly because of the effect it would make on the second eighth of measure two.

EX. 261. J. S. Bach—*Well-tempered Clavier, I, Fugue no. 18*

Inversion

Inversion at the octave would be impossible in the case of the next example. The passage would invert at two octaves. Mozart, however, has moved the upper voice down two octaves and the lower up one, making a total of three octaves, or double counterpoint at the twenty-second. This is normally called double counterpoint at the fifteenth.

EX. 262. Mozart—*Sonata, K. 498a*

Similar in range is the following combination of fugal subject and countersubject. Reference to the complete fugue will show the wide range of the texture resulting partly from this relationship of the two subjects.

EX. 263. J. S. Bach—*Well-tempered Clavier, I, Fugue no. 12*

Below are two specimens of double counterpoint in orchestral music. The pitch range is normally much wider in this medium than in writing for the keyboard, or for small groups of instruments. The idiomatic octave doublings have been omitted from these examples, since they do not affect the counterpoint as such.

In the passage from Mozart's G Minor Symphony, the pattern of

EX. 264. Beethoven—*Symphony no. 3*

EX. 265. Mozart—*Symphony, K. 550*

the first four measures is not only inverted in the four following measures but there is also a modulation to the key a major second lower.

Another use of double counterpoint is shown below. Here the bass of the antecedent part of the phrase becomes the upper melody of the consequent and vice versa.

EX. 266. J. S. Bach—*Two-part Invention no. 6*

EX. 267. J. S. Bach—*Well-tempered Clavier, II, Prelude no. 20*

Sequences are frequently constructed in double counterpoint, using comparatively short motives. In example 268 the motives change mode as well as key. The inversion is by octave and fourth up plus octave and fifth down, a total of three octaves.

EX. 268. J. S. Bach—*Well-tempered Clavier, I, Fugue no. 10*

In Haydn's Symphony no. 47, the entire slow movement is based on varied forms of the phrase in double counterpoint at the fifteenth.

EX. 269. Haydn—*Symphony no. 47*

DOUBLE COUNTERPOINT AT THE TENTH

In inversion at the tenth the harmonic intervals are changed as follows:

unison	becomes	tenth	sixth	becomes	fifth
second	"	ninth	seventh	"	fourth
third	"	octave	octave	"	third
fourth	"	seventh	ninth	"	second
fifth	"	sixth	tenth	"	unison

In this case the consonant intervals remain consonant, except that perfect consonances are exchanged for imperfect, and imperfect for perfect. Dissonances remain dissonances. Exception to both these rules is made in the case of the occasional fifth which is diminished by reason of its position in the scale.

Inversion at the tenth changes the position of the whole melody in the scale, so that its melodic intervals undergo slight changes. If the melodic intervals were kept exactly the same, a kind of bitonality would result, or at least a weakening of the fundamental tonality. On the other hand, such a melodic interval as the perfect fourth from the second degree up to the dominant becomes, a tenth higher, a tritone from the fourth up to the seventh degree. If the interval is to be used, either the melodic treatment of the perfect fourth should be such as to result in proper progression from the tritone, or one of the notes of the tritone may be altered, making it a perfect fourth.

Another peculiarity of double counterpoint at the tenth is that consecutive thirds and sixths become in the inversion consecutive fifths and octaves. Therefore all relative motion must be either contrary or oblique.

The following example is remarkable in that the countersubject, the part in sixteenths, is invertible at either the octave, the tenth, or the twelfth.

EX. 270. J. S. Bach—*Well-tempered Clavier, II, Fugue no. 16*

Inversion

The designation "double counterpoint at the tenth" is likewise applied when the inversion requires transposition of an octave more than a tenth.

EX. 271. J. S. Bach—*The Art of Fugue, Contrapunctus X*

Inversion

This fugue also illustrates the principle that double counterpoint at the tenth may be combined with double counterpoint at the octave by doubling one of the voices in thirds or sixths. The student will recog-

EX. 272

nize that this procedure does not create triple counterpoint from double but simply adds harmonic doubling to one part.

DOUBLE COUNTERPOINT AT THE TWELFTH

The inversion at the twelfth does not present as much difficulty as the inversion at the tenth, and is much more practical. The table of harmonic interval changes is as follows:

unison	becomes	twelfth	seventh	becomes	sixth
second	"	eleventh	octave	"	fifth
third	"	tenth	ninth	"	fourth
fourth	"	ninth	tenth	"	third
fifth	"	octave	eleventh	"	second
sixth	"	seventh	twelfth	"	unison

Octaves become fifths and vice versa. Thirds interchange with tenths. But the circumstance that a sixth inverts to a seventh presents an obstacle to flexibility in melodic writing.

Below are two examples of double counterpoint at the twelfth. The first shows the minimum of transposition, exactly a twelfth, while in the second the voices are moved a total of three octaves and a fifth.

EX. 273. J. S. Bach—*Well-tempered Clavier, I, Fugue no. 2*

Inversion

EX. 274. J. S. Bach—*The Art of Fugue, Contrapunctus IX*

Free parts may be added to double counterpoint. They are often helpful in clarifying the harmony and sometimes make possible certain inversions which would be questionable in the two voices by themselves. In the following example the third measure is undoubtedly improved by the addition of the free bass part.

EX. 275. Brahms—*Variations on a Theme by Haydn, op. 56a*

TRIPLE COUNTERPOINT

Three-part writing is called triple counterpoint when the order of the three voices is completely invertible. Theoretically, these six arrangements of the voices should be available:

A A B B C C
B C A C A B
C B C A B A

In practice, however, some of these combinations may be less desirable than others and, since it is rare that a composer will wish to use all the six arrangements, those are employed which are most satisfactory musically. If the three parts are truly in triple counterpoint, each of the voices will be able to serve as a bass for the others. Each pair of voices is in double counterpoint at the octave or fifteenth. The close position of the octave is to be preferred if all six inversions are wanted.

Since the inversion of a perfect fourth makes a perfect fifth, besides the dissonant character of the fourth itself, the three voices cannot at any time proceed in parallel chords of the sixth. Other difficulties arise from the presence of the note of resolution simultaneously with a dissonance like the suspension or the appoggiatura. But these apparent obstacles can be modified by so many different circumstances that the experimental method remains the best way to work out this type of counterpoint, as indeed it has been seen to be with all other types.

The following is an example showing the practical application of triple counterpoint. The entire prelude consists of phrases which are inversions of the first phrase, with a few additional episodic measures of transition and coda. Four of the six possible arrangements are employed, and these are shown here. Note the minor changes made in B and C.

EX. 276. J. S. Bach—*Well-tempered Clavier, I, Prelude no. 19*

Triple counterpoint is frequently found in the episodes of the fugue, where the passage is often based on a sequence, and each thematic fragment appears in turn as upper, middle, and lower voice. Such passages are also used in other forms of composition, like the sonata, for purposes of transition and development.

EX. 277. J. S. Bach—*Well-tempered Clavier, II, Fugue no. 17*

QUADRUPLE COUNTERPOINT

In a strict sense, a phrase cannot be said to be in quadruple counterpoint unless all twenty-four of the possible variants prove successful as four-part counterpoint. Needless to say, the test is rarely made. If each of the four voices will work as a suitable bass for the other three, the counterpoint will suffice as quadruple counterpoint for most musical purposes.

Two positions of a phrase in quadruple counterpoint are given in the example below. The soprano, marked A, has in the inversion been placed in the bass, while the order of the other three voices has been preserved, B, C, D.

If the student has curiosity to investigate the other inversions of this specimen of quadruple counterpoint he will discover that some are less practicable than others. The line marked B does not, in fact, make as good a bass as the other voices do, which may be a reason why Bach did not use that inversion in the fugue. However, its dominant pedal quality cannot be said to disqualify the part as a possible bass.

EX. 278. J. S. Bach—*Well-tempered Clavier, I, Fugue no. 12*

Inversion

Although the writing of canons is not the immediate concern of studies in invertible counterpoint one natural result of the practical presentation of triple or quadruple counterpoint is the formation of canons. If a short pattern is so constructed as to be invertible the composer will doubtless wish to display several of its inversions, and if these are presented so that the melodic patterns appear in the same order of succession in all the voices a canon will be created. The effectiveness of the canon will depend upon the degree of excellence of the melodic line made by the succession of melodic units.

Three variants appear in the next illustration, a sequence in quadruple counterpoint. Should the melodic units A, B, C, D, in this kind of sequence, follow one another in the same order in each voice, a four-part canon would be formed. Here, for instance, the middle voice shows the start of such a canon, the melody being the succession of motives C, D, A, B. The second voice of the canon would be the bass, and if the sequence were prolonged, all four voices would eventually complete the same melodic sequence.

EX. 279. J. S. Bach—*The Musical Offering, Ricercare a 6*

QUINTUPLE COUNTERPOINT

As an example of the rare counterpoint in five invertible voices, there are shown below three inversions of the five-part counterpoint already given in example 251, in the preceding chapter. The five string parts are doubled by woodwinds and in the score there are some background notes for horns, trumpets, and timpani, here omitted.

EX. 280. Mozart—*Symphony, K. 551*

EXERCISES

In writing exercises in invertible counterpoint, it will not be necessary to carry out the exact transposition of the parts to the very last note of the phrase. As a matter of fact, in some of the combinations a satisfactory cadence is impossible of attainment without some variation in the inversions. It is therefore more practical to say that free cadences may be used.

Also, it has been remarked that variations in the melodic intervals result from new positions in the scale in the inversions at the tenth and twelfth. Advantage may be taken of this precedent to make other chromatic alterations not indicated by the scale of the key, but which improve the harmonic effect by suggesting secondary dominant harmony or change of mode.

High standards of melodic writing should be upheld at all times. The temptation to excuse a weak melodic part on the ground that the contrapuntal problem is a difficult one must be steadfastly repelled, if practice in counterpoint is to be of value in developing musical insight and flexibility.

1. Write parts in double counterpoint at the octave, tenth, twelfth, and fifteenth, to each of the following given parts. In each case show the inversion. The given parts may be transposed to other keys, on inversion, if so desired.

(a)

Andante (Mozart)

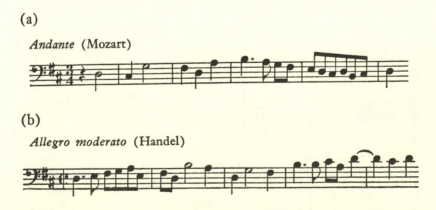

(b)

Allegro moderato (Handel)

(c)

Allegro (Mendelssohn)

(d)

Moderato (Bach)

2. Write sequences in double counterpoint on the following harmonic patterns.

(a)

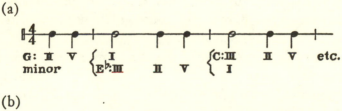

(b)

3. Construct a musical sentence of two phrases in double counterpoint in which the first phrase modulates from B minor to D major, with an authentic cadence in the latter key. The second phrase returns to B minor.

4. Write a phrase in triple counterpoint and show two inversions of the same.

5. Write a phrase in quadruple counterpoint and show one inversion.

※»《※

CANON IN TWO PARTS

E VER since the Middle Ages, composers have been attracted by the effect of reduplication of a melody by a second voice, starting a little later than the voice originally announcing the melody. The result is called a two-part canon.

The second voice may follow at any time interval and may reproduce the melody at any harmonic interval from the original. The two parts of the canon may be unaccompanied, or they may be supplemented by one or more free voices. Such added parts often help to clarify the harmony or rhythm of the canon, or they may be included simply as enrichment of the texture.

A canon may be continued throughout an entire piece, without being interrupted at cadences or modulations. The student should consult the four canons in Bach's *The Art of Fugue* with especial attention to their form and continuity. The opening measures of one of these canons are given here. The whole piece is 103 bars long.

These canons by Bach are written in double counterpoint (see page 223), and the forms are ingeniously constructed so as to present the inversions. Not only is the order of voices inverted but the melodic lines are introduced in contrary motion. Needless to say, these features are hardly discernible by the listener on a single hearing and are to be appreciated only through careful study of the music.

EX. 281. J. S. Bach—*The Art of Fugue, Canone alla Ottava*

This type of small form based on a canon is sometimes used as one of a series of variations, like those from which examples 287 and 299 are drawn. It has also been found appropriate for short movements in larger works, as for instance the Menuetto in example 282.

EX. 282. Haydn—*Quartet, op. 76, no. 2*

Allegro ma non troppo

Often one or two phrases are singled out for canonic treatment, as in the following presentation of the second theme in the first movement of Beethoven's Fourth Symphony. Notice that here the use of canon doubles the effect of rhythmic repetition in the motive structure.

EX. 283. Beethoven—*Symphony no. 4*

Canons of smaller melodic units are a common feature in the fugue. Giving out the fugue subject in canon with itself is called stretto.

EX. 284. J. S. Bach—*Well-tempered Clavier, I, Fugue no. 1*

TIME INTERVAL

If the second voice waits too long before entering, the canon is difficult for the ear to follow, especially if the canon is continued through several phrases. Moreover, as will be discovered in writing canons, it is far easier to construct one with a time interval of several measures than one with a short time interval, so that the aesthetic effect of appreciation of skill and craftsmanship is greatly lessened.

The easiest time interval to follow by ear, and the most natural, is that of one or two measures of moderate length, with the second voice in a similar metric position to the first. In the well-known canon from the Franck Violin Sonata, the beginning of which is shown below, both parts begin on the fourth quarter, a measure apart.

As two-part counterpoint this canon is weakened by the pronounced symmetrical quality of its melodic rhythm and by the excess of har-

monic agreement of the voices on the strong beats. The added voices
in the piano part are necessary on account of certain fourths in the
two-part canon, and they are used in a way to accentuate the harmonic
quality of the texture.

EX. 285. Franck—*Sonata for Violin and Piano*

The following unaccompanied canon is more subtle in its harmonic
effect, no doubt because of the use of dissonant intervals on the first
beats of four out of six measures. The absence of harmonic filling leaves
to the listener the added interest of relating the two voices to the
harmonic background implied.

EX. 286. Wilhelm Friedemann Bach—*Sonata in D Major*

Time intervals shorter than one measure call for more attentive listening although if the tempo is not fast and the interval is measured in important beats the rhythm will probably not prove confusing. Brahms gives no tempo indication for the example below, but we may assume from the character of the variation that it is not very lively, and that the four beats of each measure have an equal rhythmic importance. At any rate, the two lines do not seem to disagree metrically, except on paper. This point will be made clearer in the discussion of succeeding examples.

The harmony is noticeably static and lacking in contrapuntal quality, the entire phrase being made with but two changes of root. Contrapuntal elements are found in the opposition of the melodic curves and in some variety in the melodic rhythms.

EX. 287. Brahms—*Variations on a Theme by Handel, op. 24*

Some of the same static quality is likewise present in the following canon by Bizet. The harmony is mostly tonic throughout, but there is a feeling of half-cadence at the end of the phrase. (The final tonic chord in the example is actually the first chord of the second phrase.)

EX. 288. Bizet—*L'Arlésienne, Farandole*

The next example is extremely difficult to follow by ear, not only because the time interval is so very short but also because the two parts are not similarly placed metrically. Assuming that the melodic rhythms are identical since the melodies are identical, the second voice must be incorrectly barred, if the barring is to give any indication as to where the down-beats occur. The accompaniment offers no assistance since the chords are entirely without accent and there is no change of root to permit a suggestion by means of harmonic rhythm. In this connection the reader is advised to consult again the remarks on the subject of melodic and harmonic rhythm in previous chapters.

EX. 289. J. S. Bach—*Brandenburg Concerto no. 6*

There is the same question of a shift in metric pulse, or syncopation, in the following illustration. Here the time interval is shorter than in the Bach example, and the eighth-note value amounts to but one-third of a beat, a fast six-eight time having a pulse of two to the measure. The difference in pitch location of the two parts makes it possible, however, to hear the general canonic effect of leader and close follower. This passage is an example of the way harmonic rhythm operates to preserve a sense of metric pulse. At the third full measure and again at the fifth a change of harmonic root is clearly felt, giving a rhythmic beat not present in the melodic rhythms.

EX. 290. Mozart—*Sonata, K. 576*

HARMONIC INTERVAL

As might be expected, the commonest harmonic interval between a given note in the first voice and its reduplication in the second voice is the octave. Canons at the octave, above or below, have been seen in examples 281, 282, 283, 285, 286, 287, 288, and 290. It is naturally easier for the hearer to recognize a melody reproduced in another octave than at other intervals, and this type of canon is also easier to write. At the same time, the canon at the octave presents a problem to the composer on account of its tendency to continue indefinitely with the same harmonic root. The answering voice will call for the same harmony as the antecedent and hence will give rise to a new antecedent on the same harmony, unless the composer gives it a new harmonic interpretation, when this is needed for variety and organization of the harmonic background. The examples given show the harmonic results of this natural tendency, and they are good evidence that in writing canons the difficulties lie not so much in the writing of counterpoint as in the control and direction of the harmony.

When the second voice replies at an interval other than the octave or unison, the harmonic problem is different. Transposition of the melody brings about a change of harmony, so that the tendency to static harmony is not present. The difficulty is in the control of this harmonic variety. The tones making up the first voice must be chosen with a view to producing the desired harmony when they are transposed to the second voice.

Shifting the melody to a new position in the scale also alters the size of some of the melodic intervals. Just as in the transpositions of invertible counterpoint, advantage may be taken of this circumstance to make other alterations not called for by the scale of the key but suggested by secondary dominant harmony, or change of mode.

The following canon at the fifth below, between soprano and bass, is to be studied for the variations in melodic intervals brought about by both the transposition and the skill of the composer in forming changes of harmony. Compare the tones used with the normal scale degrees expected.

Also to be noted is the balance of emphasis on the tonal degrees in the two melodies. Since the tonic will be answered a fifth lower by the subdominant, care must be taken not to allow this degree to be so strongly represented that the subdominant key is implied rather than the tonic key. Likewise if prominent dominant notes are desired in the bass, they must be created by giving prominence to the supertonic in the upper voice.

The contributions made by the free inner voices to the harmonic sonority and the contrapuntal texture should be carefully examined. For instance, in the fifth full measure the interpretation of the E in the upper voice as a harmonic seventh is made clear by the inside voices, which at the same time show the B in the bass to be an anticipation of the bass in the next measure. The D in the second violin is an appoggiatura with implied resolution to C-sharp.

EX. 291. J. S. Bach—*Suite no. 2, Sarabande*

Following are two more canons at the fifth below, both accompanied in pure harmonic fashion, in contrast to the contrapuntal texture of the accompanying voices in the Bach Sarabande.

EX. 292. Haydn—*Quartet, op. 1, no. 3*

EX. 293. Handel—*Sonata for Two Violins with Figured Bass, no. 2*

In the next illustration the canon is written at the fifth above, so that tonic is answered by dominant. Harmonic variety is gained here by

answering the seventh degree first by the subdominant, the scale degree
a fifth higher, and then by the raised subdominant, leading-tone of the
dominant.

EX. 294. J. S. Bach—*Chorale Prelude, Kyrie, Gott Vater in Ewigkeit*

If the answering voice reproduces the melodic intervals exactly, except in the canon at the octave or unison, there will be a suggestion of
two keys, or as in the following canon at the fourth below, the two
parts together will give an impression of indecision as to tonal center.

This canon is broken at the last eighth of the second full measure, and
the group of sixteenths is answered at the unison instead of at the fourth.

EX. 295. J. S. Bach—*Chorale Prelude, Wir Christenleut'*

Bach has written canons at all intervals in the set of thirty variations
known as the Goldberg Variations. This work should be studied by all
who are interested in this form of counterpoint. Below are quoted the
opening measures of two of the canons, at the third below and the
sixth above. In the first of these, a firm tonality is secured by the start
with a figure based mainly on the third and fifth degrees, since the
answer will then give tonic harmony. In the canon at the sixth, it is
plain that the two parts form a fundamental succession of parallel
sixths, to which a certain amount of rhythmic variety has been given.

EX. 296. J. S. Bach—*Goldberg Variations, Canone alla Terza*

EX. 297. J. S. Bach—*Goldberg Variations, Canone alla Sesta*

An unusual interval of transposition is that of the seventh. Following is a canon at the seventh above, the tonic being answered by the leading-tone. No chromatic alterations are used here; the scale degrees throughout are only those of B-flat minor. The time interval is close, and the answering voice enters on a different metric beat from that of the leader.

EX. 298. J. S. Bach—*Well-tempered Clavier, II, Fugue no. 22*

Canons at smaller harmonic intervals are more difficult to work out. In the canon at the second, crossing of the voices becomes necessary in carrying out the melodic curves. Usually, it will be found practical to begin the canon at the second at not too short a time interval.

Compare measures eight and ten of the following canon at the second above, with respect to alterations of the scale degrees.

EX. 299. Brahms—*Variations on a Theme by Schumann, op. 9*

Canon at the unison is the most difficult of the harmonic intervals. To the close position of the voices is added the harmonic problem of variety mentioned in connection with the canon at the octave. Since both voices have the same pitch location there is no upper or lower part.

EX. 300. J. S. Bach—*Goldberg Variations, Canone all'Unisono*

CONTRARY MOTION

In some canons the answering voice states the melody in contrary motion, moving down when the leader moves up, and vice versa. This is called canon in contrary motion, canon in inversion, or inverted canon. The first of these terms has the merit of avoiding the possible confusion of melodic inversion with inversion of the order of the voices, as in double counterpoint.

The canon in contrary motion presents no new problems, although some difference in conditions is brought about through the choice of the point of departure of the inversion. Upon this choice depend the changes in melodic intervals and whatever changes may occur in emphasis on tonal or modal scale degrees. The latter consideration is of more importance than the question of melodic intervals. Especially is it of little significance in contrary motion whether a major second is answered by a major or a minor second.

One should know what are the normal, or expected, scale degrees to answer a given melody, and for this purpose the following types of contrary motion are established. In practice, however, it will be found useful and advisable to take advantage of effective chromatic changes which may be introduced for better and more interesting harmonic organization. (See the remarks bearing on this point on page 195, likewise its application in Ex. 291).

EX. 301

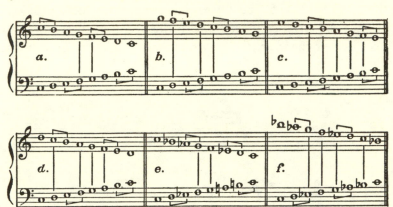

The above scheme shows the relationships between scales moving in contrary motion from various points of departure. These different types of contrary motion possess certain noteworthy characteristics affecting canonic writing.

Type I (ex. 301, *a*). Tonic is answered by tonic, dominant by subdominant, subdominant by dominant. This makes a good balance of tonality. The two scales are not related symmetrically, since their half-steps do not occur at the same points in both. (Half-steps are indicated by brackets)

Type II (ex. 301, *b*). Tonic and dominant interchange. Subdominant is answered by second degree. This is probably the most frequently used type of melodic inversion.

Type III (ex. 301, *c*). The half-steps coincide. Tonic is answered by third degree, subdominant and dominant by seventh and sixth degrees. This is not as satisfactory for tonal unity but has features of symmetry to recommend it.

Type IV (ex. 301, *d*). These two scales are balanced on their dominants, although the answering of tonic by second degree may prove inconvenient.

Type V (ex. 301, *e*). This is the version of *a* in the minor mode. The correspondence of tonal degrees remains unchanged. There are, of course, variants in the forms of the minor scales.

Type VI (ex. 301, *f*). This inversion is sometimes recommended as giving a true melodic inversion in the minor mode, because of the correspondence of whole and half-steps. The balance of tonal degrees is not very satisfactory, however.

These are the commonest inversions used, but other types can be found or invented by answering the tonic by other scale degrees, and by mixture of major and minor modes. (See example 307)

EX. 302. J. S. Bach—*Goldberg Variations, Canone alla Quarta*

Type II

EX. 303. J. S. Bach—*The Art of Fugue, Contrapunctus V*

Type II

EX. 304. J. S. Bach—*Well-tempered Clavier, II, Fugue no. 22*

An unusual type, in which tonic is answered by subdominant.

EX. 305. J. S. Bach—*Well-tempered Clavier, I, Fugue no. 6*

Type II (minor mode)

In this example the original subject is in the middle voice, the inversion leading in the upper part. A certain parallelism is avoided by delaying the resolution of the suspension E, in measure two. In the bass of the last measure Bach substitutes F-sharp for the F, which could perfectly well be used, but which would not bring about the preferred harmonic change.

EX. 306. Mozart—*Adagio for Two Bassett Horns and Bassoon, K. 410*

Type II

Mozart's notation of the answer to the progression in measure seven of the above example shows him to be most scrupulous as to the literal inversion of the melody. The rising chromatic figure in measure nine will, however, be heard as F-sharp, G, G-sharp, A, no matter how written, since the prevailing mode is major.

EX. 307. J. S. Bach—*Well-tempered Clavier, I, Fugue no. 6*

If this canon is felt to have as its tonal center A (with modulation to D), it is based on the second type of inversion. If, on the other hand, the key is D throughout (a more logical diagnosis), the tonic D is answered by the raised submediant B-natural. This is an unusual correspondence of scales, and it is not included in our six types.

METHOD

The steps in the writing of a canon may be outlined as follows:

1. Compose the opening measure or two, in one voice.

2. Copy this much in the second voice, transposing it according to the harmonic interval desired, starting at the time interval selected, or at whatever time interval seems most effective. If the time interval is less than the length of the first fragment written, some changes may have to be made in that part. Further changes back and forth between the two parts may appear advisable before continuing the canon. Be sure that in its final form the second voice is a true reproduction of the first, except for possible chromatic alterations in canons other than octave or unison.

3. Write the second fragment of the first voice, in counterpoint to the second voice, keeping in mind the resulting harmonic background and the development of the melodic line. The canon will be more effective musically if the line contains well-defined motives, which will be heard alternately in the two voices.

4. Continue these two steps throughout the phrase. Care should be taken that the third fragment in the first voice is not a replica of the first fragment, as this leads to a mechanical alternation and symmetry which become overemphasized by the double appearances in the canon.

The ideal result is a phrase in which melodic lines, harmonic organization, and counterpoint, are no less perfect because the whole happens to be a canon.

EXERCISES

1. Write a set of canons, each one phrase long, at the harmonic intervals listed below. Use two instrumental voices, with no additional voices. Include in the set as much variety in rhythmic, melodic, and harmonic styles as possible. Employ different motives in the different canons, so that each will have its musical individuality.

(a) octave above	(h) fifth below
(b) octave below	(i) fourth above
(c) seventh above	(j) fourth below
(d) seventh below	(k) third above
(e) sixth above	(l) third below
(f) sixth below	(m) second above
(g) fifth above	(n) second below

(o) unison

2. Write a two-part canon three phrases long, at the fifth above, with one additional free part.

3. Write a two-part canon at a time interval of one half measure in four-four time. Length at least one phrase.

4. Write a two-part canon at the ninth above with a free bass, for violin, viola, and violoncello. Length optional.

5. Write two-part unaccompanied canons in contrary motion, using each of the types of contrary motion shown in example 301.

❯❯❯ ❮❮❮

CHAPTER ELEVEN

OTHER TYPES OF CANON

WITH three and four voices in canon the variations in respect to time interval and harmonic interval become practically endless. The relationship between the second and third entering voices is not necessarily the same as between the first and second voices. Furthermore, the third voice is in canon with the first voice as well

EX. 308. Beethoven—*Sonata for Violin and Piano, op. 96*

208

as with its immediate partner. These complications are of course greatly multiplied if more voices are added in canon.

The three-part canon is easily followed by the hearer if the time intervals are not too close or too distant and the parts are rhythmically distinguishable. In example 308 there is in addition the wide difference in pitch between the three voices and the contrast in instrumental sound. The harmonic intervals of the canon are unison and octave.

The next example has the same harmonic intervals but a slightly closer time interval. The three voices are more clearly differentiated at the third entry of the canon than in the Beethoven excerpt, in which the two top voices find themselves in rhythmic agreement after measure eight.

EX. 309. J. S. Bach—*Organ Sonata no. 5*

The difference in pitch between adjacent voices in a three-part texture is quite likely to be less than an octave. The alternation of pitch locations on tonic and dominant is typical of the fugue, especially in the exposition. In the following canonic exposition it will be noticed that the very first melodic interval is changed from a second to a third in the second voice. This is not the result of caprice on the part of the composer but represents the observance of certain conventions of tonal balance in the fugue.

EX. 310. J. S. Bach—*Organ Fugue in C Major*

Close time intervals create an impression of intensity and excitement. This is often desired in the concentrated texture of fugal episodes, as in the following passage by Handel. Here the three-part canon is at the octave, and the effect is heightened by the further imitation of motives in the separate parts, as though more voices were entering at a fourth above.

EX. 311. Handel—*Suite no. 6, Fuga*

Below are shown the first measures of two canons by Mozart. These were written to be sung, with words, and are given here simply to show the disposition of the voices, since discussion of the effect on counterpoint of the articulation of words and the vocal style is not among the

objectives of this book. The first is a canon at the unison. In the second
the leading voice is in the middle, the canons being at the second above
and sixth below.

EX. 312. Mozart—*Canon, K. 229*

EX. 313. Mozart—*Canon, K. 508*

The canon in several voices can create a special kind of texture without necessarily having to be heard as a canon. The following phrase is
based on a three-part canon, at the seventh, then the fifth, below. But
the harmonic nature of the texture, with added tones often making five
parts, and the absence of rhythmic independence in the counterpoint,
make it clear that the three lines of the canon serve rather as unifying
threads than as important voices to be followed through by player and
listener in order to understand the music. The cadences, half-way
through and at the end, are free.

Compare example 315 with example 311. The time interval is the
same, but there are four parts instead of three and the intervals between

EX. 314. Schumann—*Canon, "An Alexis"*

EX. 315. J. S. Bach—*The Art of Fugue, Contrapunctus V*

the leading voice and the second, third, and fourth voices are respectively octave, fourth, and eleventh. This gives a balance of tonality through the alternation of tonic and dominant.

This tonal balance is important in all canonic writing and it has been seen that its security depends largely upon the relative emphasis of tonal degrees. In the example below, the motive itself begins with dominant and tonic. The canons are at the octave above and octave below, with a third entry in contrary motion which answers dominant by tonic and vice versa. The time intervals are a half measure, one measure and a half, and one measure. It will be noticed that the canon is not strictly carried out, but is simulated by imitation of motives so that it is very difficult to tell by ear that it is not a true canon throughout.

EX. 316. Mozart—*Fugue for Two Pianos, K. 426*

The two illustrations which follow have four entries on the same scale degrees, fifth, third, first, and sixth. Note the influence of this on the impression of tonality. Also compare the two canons as contrasts in the effect of long and short time intervals.

EX. 317. J. S. Bach—*Well-tempered Clavier, II, Fugue no. 5*

EX. 318. Klengel—*Canons and Fugues, I, Canone XV*

DOUBLE CANON

The four-part texture lends itself to division into two two-part canons. In example 319 the canon in eighth-note triplets acts as accompaniment to the canon in longer notes, and the two canons are well differentiated. In example 320, on the other hand, the two canons in contrary motion, although distinguishable in that the second pair of voices starts later than the first and lies in a different register, seem to be related thematically and to be of equal musical importance.

EX. 319. J. S. Bach—*Chorale Prelude, In dulci jubilo*

Hence the double canon may have these two aspects. It may consist of a canon accompanied by another, relatively subordinate, canon. Or it may consist of a balanced four-part texture in which the two canons have an equal share of the significant motives of the phrase.

EX. 320. Mozart—*String Quintet, K. 406*

Minuetto in canone

The following double canon on an ostinato bass, by Bach, is remarkable for the richness of the harmony, and for the ingenious placing of the voices in respect to spacing and rhythm.

EX. 321. J. S. Bach—*Double Canon upon an Ostinato Bass*

FIVE-PART CANON

Canons in more than four voices lose their effectiveness after a few measures because of the difficulty of following their complexities by ear. Some of the parts need to be subordinated to the extent of making them mere holding tones, or giving them rests, if continuity of musical thought is to be preserved. Otherwise the result may have value only as texture, or harmonic sonority. Such canons are not usually continued for long after each voice has entered with the principal motive.

EX. 322. Mozart—*Quintet for Horn, Violin, Two Violas, and 'Cello, K. 407*

In the works of Mozart the student will find canons for as many as six voices (K. 347), as well as a triple canon for three four-part choruses (K. 348).

If the second voice of the canon is written in notes twice as long as the values in the first voice we have a canon in augmentation. The values may be augmented in some other ratio but doubling is by far the most common. As can be seen in the example given below, the time intervals of this canon grow progressively longer, so that after a few beats the original melody is so far outdistanced by its augmented imitation that the problem of canonic writing is greatly simplified. The peculiar consideration in this type of canon is that of harmonic organization. This must be carefully planned in the first voice so that the slowing down of the root movements by augmentation does not produce a static feeling in the harmonic rhythm, especially at points where a strong root progression should normally occur.

EX. 323. J. S. Bach—*Chorale Variations, Vom Himmel hoch*

Canons of shorter melodic units, such as fugue subjects, can sometimes be arranged so that the augmentation extends through two statements of the theme in origin l form. In the following illustration the augmentation appears first as a canon at the octave above. When the first voice completes its statement of the subject, the part in augmentation becomes the first voice of a new canon at the fourth above.

EX. 324. J. S. Bach—*Well-tempered Clavier, I, Fugue no. 8*

EX. 325. J. S. Bach—*The Art of Fugue, Canon per Augmentationem, contrario motu*

This canon combines augmentation with the principle of contrary motion. Tonic is answered by dominant. The entire canon is written in double counterpoint, so that a repetition of the 52 measure canon, inverting the order of voices, makes a small two-part form.

CANON IN DIMINUTION

Diminution, the second voice in values half as long as the leader, offers a different problem from that of augmentation, since the time interval, instead of growing longer, gets rapidly shorter. In fact, the leading voice, after a few beats, finds itself in the position of follower, and the canon becomes one of augmentation. Below is an example of a three-part canon with diminution in two voices. The second voice is also in contrary motion.

EX. 326. J. S. Bach—*The Art of Fugue, Contrapunctus VI*

In diminution as well as in augmentation the variation in note values may be by another ratio than two to one. Here is an instance of diminution in which the values are reduced to one-third the original length, a natural division in six-eight meter.

EX. 327. Brahms—*Sonata, op. 5*

Allegro moderato

In the following example the middle voice is imitated in augmentation by the bass, and in diminution by the upper part.

EX. 328. Klengel—*Canons and Fugues, I, Canone VI*

CRAB CANON

The canon by retrograde motion, otherwise called crab canon, or *canon cancrizans*, is more an intellectual stunt than a purely musical effect. It is perhaps the best known and most typical of that large category of musical puzzles or tests of ingenuity in which musicians have always taken great delight, even though the results may have little to say as musical expression.

Solution of contrapuntal problems of this kind usually means satisfying the conditions given, while producing something recognizable as music, and this part of the contrapuntal tradition can have value in the development of contrapuntal facility, provided high musical standards are maintained. At the same time, it must be admitted that the skill and artistry thus exhibited are to be appreciated more by seeing than by hearing.

In the crab canon the melody is accompanied by itself played backwards. An example of this type, quoted below in full, is to be found in *The Musical Offering*, by Bach. Notice that the voices inevitably cross at the central point, the bar between measures nine and ten, and that here there is of necessity a repetition of the G and the B-flat across the bar-line. Since measure ten is the retrograde form of measure nine, it follows that the first notes of the former must be the same as the last notes of the latter.

EX. 329. J. S. Bach—*The Musical Offering, Retrograde Canon*

MIRROR

Although not strictly a canon, the "mirror" may be described as a canon in contrary motion at a time interval of zero. The procedure is shown in the example below, in soprano and bass. Each interval of the upper melody is copied in contrary motion by the bass.

EX. 330. Brahms—*Variations on a Theme by Schumann, op. 9*

The intervals in the above example are exactly reproduced in the inversion. Different positions in the scale may, however, cause slight alterations in the intervals, as in the following passage from a Bach fugue. Here the inversion is that in which tonic is answered by dominant, compared to tonic answered by mediant in example 330.

EX. 331. J. S. Bach—*Well-tempered Clavier, II, Fugue no. 8*

The term mirror is also used for the inversion of the whole of the music, both the melodies and the order of the voices. The famous mirror fugue in *The Art of Fugue* (*Contrapunctus XII*) is constructed so that not only the order of the voices but the melodic lines themselves may be played in inversion. The whole is not intended to sound together as eight-part counterpoint, and no canonic combination is involved.

CANON IN DOUBLE COUNTERPOINT

Canons may be written in any of the types of double counterpoint. This principle is used as the basis of the canonic pieces in *The Art of Fugue*. The beginning of the canon in double counterpoint at the tenth is shown in example 332. The second half of the piece begins as in example 333. The second half is exactly like the first half except that the upper voice is now a tenth lower, and the lower voice has been transposed up an octave to become the upper voice.

EX. 332. J. S. Bach—*The Art of Fugue, Canone alla Decima*

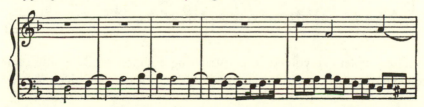

EX. 333

Canons are sometimes composed to sound with a given part, such as a chorale tune or other *cantus firmus*. Probably the most famous example of this technical procedure is the set of variations for organ on the chorale, "Vom Himmel hoch," by Bach. One of the variations is given below.

EX. 334. J. S. Bach—*Chorale Variations, Vom Himmel hoch*

The problems involved in constructing a canon while at the same time meeting the conditions imposed by the presence of a given melody furnish excellent practice for the development of contrapuntal technique, and exercises of this type are strongly recommended.

PERPETUAL CANON

The perpetual, or infinite, canon is one in which the leading voice repeats its first measure at what would be the final cadential measure, thus leading to an endless repetition of the canon. It does not present serious technical difficulties and is usually looked upon as a stunt. There is, nevertheless, a practical use for this kind of cadence. Occasionally one wishes to repeat a phrase written in canon, in which case the first ending is arranged as for a perpetual canon.

ENIGMA CANON

In the enigma, or riddle, canon only one part is written out, leaving the players to discover the time interval, or the harmonic interval, or both, at which the second voice may enter in canon. Often some signs or hints are given to help in the solution, so that there is really no riddle about it, but the term is usually applied to all canons the parts of which are not written out.

Needless to say, what matters is the music and how it sounds, not any ingenuities in its notation. The enigma canon was, however, very popular among musicians in the eighteenth century. The double canon shown in example 320 was written by Bach as an enigma canon. The entire canon, together with solutions to other riddle canons by Bach, and an excellent discussion of this subject, may be found in the *Bach Reader*, by Hans T. David and Arthur Mendel (W. W. Norton and Co., 1945). Other canons of this type are to be seen in *The Musical Offering*, by Bach.

The following is an example of the original notation of one of these canons, with its solution in four voices.

EX. 335. J. S. Bach—*Infinite Canon in Four Parts*

METHOD

The student will readily perceive that directions for a procedure in writing the types of canon described in this chapter would be of considerable complexity. Moreover, they would have to take the form of an analysis of mental steps in the exercise of ingenuity in the manipulation of notes, many of which steps can safely be assumed to be at once apparent to one who has acquired and practiced the knowledge of the principles presented in the foregoing chapters. It seems, then, more practical and realistic to say to the student that he is on his own in the solution of these problems. In addition to the knowledge and experience he may possess he will need patience, perseverance, and the strong will to succeed. The final word of advice must be that however complex the problem, he should not take satisfaction in its solution unless the result is of high standards as pure music. The real test is how it sounds. It is hoped that these standards have been amply indicated by the examples offered in this book.

EXERCISES

Write canons of the following types, one phrase in length.

1. Three parts, time interval one measure, the second voice an octave above the first, the third voice an octave below the first.

2. Three parts, time interval two measures, the second voice a fifth above the first, the third voice an octave above the first.

3. Three parts, one in contrary motion, harmonic and time intervals optional.

4. Four parts, intervals optional.

5. Four parts, double canon, the two two-part canons differentiated as to motives used.

6. Four parts, double canon, two separate canons but with the same thematic content.

7. Two parts, one in augmentation.

8. Two parts, one in diminution.

9. Two parts, crab canon.

10. Two parts, mirror.

11. A set of two-part canons, at all harmonic intervals (*see* Chapter Ten, exercise 1), each superposed on the following *cantus firmus* as a bass. The bass may be transposed for variety.

THE evolution of musical style which brought so many radical changes in the idioms of twentieth century composers could not affect the underlying principles of counterpoint. The elements of agreement and disagreement remain true criteria for the evaluation of the contrapuntal quality of any music. The student, with a good understanding of the interplay of these elements in the music of the eighteenth and nineteenth centuries, is prepared to investigate their reaction upon music of more modern times.

It is worth repeating that virtually all music has some contrapuntal quality, and that no music is entirely contrapuntal, to our ears. We have seen that, in the historical periods we have been considering, the harmonic element, popularly conceived as the opposite of contrapuntal, makes important contributions to counterpoint, that it is, in fact, itself a contrapuntal element.

Although now nearly half the century has passed, and music of its early years can no longer be called modern, the twentieth century cannot be said to have shown a common practice in either harmony or counterpoint. The principles of common practice of the preceding period still constitute the norm by reference to which the divergences of individual practices may be appraised.

The terms "free counterpoint" and "linear music" have been employed from time to time to describe a texture in which the melodic lines do not seem to be related to a common harmony. In many of these cases the harmonic background will be discovered through closer study and through the adoption of a broader concept of harmony. But a substantial amount of this music really has no formal harmonic background.

When no harmonic organization can be perceived, the contrapuntal

228

quality of the music rests upon the independence of the melodic rhythms and of the melodic curves. Under these conditions the composer must find a substitute for the harmonic rhythm, which was so useful as a foil to contrapuntal melodies and so helpful to the hearer through its indications of a metric pulse. The latter function of harmonic rhythm is especially valuable in counterpoint since it relieves the melodic lines of the responsibility of indicating meter.

The composer's efforts, conscious or unconscious, to supply the qualities lost through the absence of harmonic rhythm have resulted in many cases in an identification of melodic accents with the down-beats of a metric pulse, and this in turn has led to the exploitation of irregular meters and even to the elimination of the bar-lines, in a few instances. This is, of course, not the sole influence behind the use of irregularity of metric pulse, but it is an important one. It should be added that these limitations have not prevented the creation of significant music.

A deep interest in rhythm for itself has had its effect on counterpoint. Using percussion instruments alone, the contrast of rhythmic patterns gives a counterpoint of rhythms lacking only the harmony and melodic curves of counterpoint as we are accustomed to speak of it. Percussive accents are also created with dissonant harmonic sonorities not meant to be identified as chords.

The melodic rhythms have been developed by modern composers with great freedom and flexibility. When combined in counterpoint they often reach a high degree of complexity and independence. Polyrhythms, such as three against four, and three against five, are employed, and experiments have been made in the notation of rhythm by placing the bar-lines at different points in different melodies, in an effort to make clear the independent down-beats. Solution of the problem of notation of rhythm is one of the greatest needs at present, and there can be no doubt that development of the technique of counterpoint in the direction of the combination of free melodic lines is being seriously retarded by the problem of notation.

The development of harmony in the nineteenth and early twentieth centuries worked to the disadvantage of counterpoint. Composers became predominantly interested in the vertical sonorities, whether these had been created by contrapuntal means or built by superposition of intervals. Gradually all contrapuntal dissonances became harmonic dissonances and the forward tendency of dissonance was much weakened, and at times entirely lost.

Hence by the growth of harmonic dissonance one of the important elements of disagreement, that between a melody and its harmony, became comparatively ineffective. The nonharmonic tones themselves became chord members. It is a commonplace in speaking of early twentieth century harmony to explain a chord as being partly composed of unresolved nonharmonic tones.

Efforts to create dissonance for rhythmic and dynamic purposes in a harmonic texture whose basis was already dissonant soon reached the limit of our small number of semitones. Composers then began treating dissonances as consonances, so that all tones were available harmonically at any given moment. Thus the contrapuntal characteristic of disagreement was completely lost, as far as harmony is concerned.

Counterpoint makes its own harmony, as we have seen. In this way the tapestry of sound produced by the melodic weaving of voices in a convention like pandiatonism or the twelve-tone system creates expressive and sometimes fascinating harmony, but this harmony lacks organization, particularly rhythmic organization, and the counterpoint is less effective for its lack of contrapuntal relationship to a harmonic background.

Polytonality is contrapuntal in its effect, because of the opposition of tonal centers. Two melodies in different keys are certainly independent to that extent. A counterpoint of harmonic streams, two contrapuntal voices each with its individual harmony, is related to this procedure. Chord streams of parallel triads or other chords, moving in different directions, have been used with some success. This may be compared to the classic procedure of doubling two contrapuntal lines in thirds.

Modern composers have used the contrapuntal devices of canon, inversion, and mirror writing. Their effectiveness depends upon the harmonic style adopted for the particular work. If it is a style in which all notes are regarded as consonant together, it is obvious that the contrapuntal combinations pose no problem of technique for the composer.

Students who have completed the studies outlined in this book should be prepared to approach the music of the twentieth century with an understanding of the contrapuntal aspects it presents, whether this approach is made from the standpoint of composer, performer, teacher, or musicologist. The author has not tried to establish or perfect an individual style, or to determine minutely the proper conduct of individual notes in counterpoint. He has intended to present the principles by which the contrapuntal element has operated in the works of composers in the belief that these principles will have lasting validity in any instrumental music based on harmony and rhythm.

INDEX

Accent, 26, 33, 46, 54, 69, 88, 114, 125, 130, 193, 229
Altered chords, 43
Anacrusis, 33, 39, 50, 99
Antecedent, 37, 174
Anticipation, 48, 51, 53
Appoggiatura, 32, 33, 39, 44, 46, 49, 51, 56, 58, 59, 86, 152, 180
Augmentation, 80, 103, 153, 218, 220
Augmented intervals, 89
Augmented sixth, 44
Auxiliary, 55, 59, 82, 88

Bach, C. P. E., 49, 77, 132
Bach, J. C., 15, 54
Bach, J. S., 10, 11, 12, 14, 15, 16, 17, 23, 27, 28, 38, 43, 45, 46, 48, 53, 54, 58, 62, 76, 78, 82, 84, 87, 91, 92, 94, 95, 96, 101, 103, 104, 106, 110, 113, 114, 116, 119, 125, 126, 129, 130, 135, 136, 138, 141, 146, 148, 150, 153, 154, 155, 158, 161, 165, 166, 174, 184, 187, 193, 196, 198, 199, 201, 203, 209, 210, 215, 216, 218, 222, 224, 225
   Well-tempered Clavier, I, 14, 16, 33, 36, 55, 58, 63, 67, 72, 87, 94, 103, 108, 126, 133, 151, 152, 160, 170, 171, 172, 175, 178, 181, 183, 190, 204, 205, 219
   Well-tempered Clavier, II, 60, 84, 87, 93, 108, 127, 131, 174, 176, 182, 200, 204, 214, 223
   The Art of Fugue, 37, 39, 53, 73, 81, 91, 97, 123, 145, 151, 165, 169, 177, 179, 189, 203, 212, 219, 220, 224
Bach, W. F., 192
Beethoven, 42, 103
   Quartets, 14, 62, 69, 79, 92, 97, 100, 134, 144, 150
   Sonatas, 33, 35, 49, 51, 75, 76, 77, 88, 109, 120, 123, 128, 208
   Symphonies, 29, 31, 36, 39, 73, 128, 146, 170, 173, 190
Berlioz, 32, 80

Bizet, 193
Brahms, 19, 31, 34, 38, 46, 61, 79, 85, 94, 101, 102, 104, 106, 107, 133, 156, 179, 192, 200, 220, 222
Bruckner, 20, 37

Cadence, 186, 188, 211
Canon, 112, 183, 208, 230
Canon in augmentation, 218
Canon in diminution, 220
Canon in double counterpoint, 223
Cantus firmus, 224
Cambiata, 55, 59, 94
Changing-tones, 57
Chopin, 15, 27, 39, 56, 65, 75
Chord-line melody, 42
Chromatic alteration, 186, 199, 206
Chromatic chords, 59
Chromaticism, 43, 91, 128
Compound curve, 23
Consecutive fifths, 83, 147, 176
Consecutive octaves, 83, 146, 176
Consequent, 174
Contrapuntal dissonance, 45, 90, 229
Contrary motion, 78, 83, 103, 113, 156, 167, 201, 213, 214, 219, 222
Corelli, 97
Crab canon, 221
Cross relation, 94, 125
Crossing of voices, 81, 134, 152, 170, 200, 221

Delayed resolution, 52, 126
Diminished intervals, 89
Diminution, 103, 220
Direct fifth, 86, 125, 146
Direct octave, 86, 125, 146
Dissonance, 44, 51, 58, 63, 75, 87, 89, 125, 151, 176, 229
Diminished seventh chord, 43
Dominant seventh chord, 127
Dominant ninth chord, 44, 51
Double auxiliary, 57

Double canon, 214, 225
Double counterpoint, 167, 201, 219, 223
  at the octave, 168
  at the tenth, 175
  at the twelfth, 178
  at the fifteenth, 171
Doubling, 83, 85, 89, 95, 126, 143, 145, 148, 158, 177, 230
Down-beat, 30, 33, 39, 47, 51, 64, 99, 193, 229

Echappée, 55, 59, 84
Eleventh chord, 45, 52, 130
Enigma canon, 225

Figured bass, 41, 74
Five-part canon, 216
Five-part counterpoint, 157
Four-part counterpoint, 143, 182
Franck, 47, 89, 92, 124, 191
Free counterpoint, 228
Fugue, 108, 118, 169, 172, 181, 190, 209, 218, 223

Grieg, 100

Handel, 22, 35, 38, 42, 57, 74, 86, 111, 112, 120, 122, 129, 141, 144, 186, 197, 210
Harmonic activity, 62, 130
Harmonic background, 40, 62, 72, 75, 94, 122, 127, 191, 194, 206, 228, 230
Harmonic dissonance, 44, 51, 59, 63, 126, 131, 229
Harmonic interval, 194, 208
Harmonic minor, 92
Harmonic progression, 127
Harmonic relationships, 88
Harmonic rhythm, 27, 42, 51, 60, 63, 95, 158, 193, 218, 228
Haydn, Quartets, 18, 21, 28, 50, 68, 101, 102, 109, 121, 147, 157, 189, 197
  Sonatas, 57, 67, 131
  Symphonies, 85, 107, 114, 127, 175
Hidden fifths, 86
Hidden octaves, 86

Infinite canon, 225
Inversion, 81, 104, 113, 153, 167, 201, 223, 230
Invertible counterpoint, 167, 195
Imitation, 110, 123, 147, 153, 158, 210, 213

Klengel, 214, 221

Leading-tone, 94, 95, 199
Linear music, 228
Liszt, 56

Melodic activity, 36, 37, 158
Melodic curve, 13, 72, 74, 77, 95, 108, 121, 130, 144, 228
Melodic minor, 92
Melodic rhythm, 26, 42, 63, 68, 95, 114, 145, 190, 228
Melodic skip, 19, 31, 56, 87
Melodic unit, 21, 35, 94, 99, 190
Mendelssohn, 16, 34, 57, 122, 149, 187
Meter, 26, 35, 38, 63, 68, 229
Metric relationships, 63
Mirror, 222, 230
Modal degrees, 95, 126, 145, 201
Mode, 41, 95, 186
Modulation, 41, 173, 188, 206
Motive, 35, 99, 147, 153, 206, 213
Motive structure, 99, 123
Motive variation, 103
Mozart, 15, 22, 35, 44, 66, 100, 106, 111, 131, 149, 160, 186, 205, 211, 213, 217, 218
  Quartets, 19, 20, 33, 85, 90, 112, 124, 137, 154
  Sonatas, 32, 74, 86, 88, 111, 113, 116, 148, 172, 194
  Symphonies, 51, 70, 159, 173, 185

Neapolitan sixth, 43
Ninth chord, 45, 52, 63
Nonessential tones, 45
Nonharmonic tones, 19, 43, 45, 51, 52, 53, 58, 86, 90, 230

Ornamental resolution, 58, 59
Overlapping voices, 82

Palestrina, 10
Pandiatonism, 230
Parallel motion, 83, 120
Passing-tone, 44, 47, 48, 53, 56, 78, 86, 88, 106
Pedal, 69
Perpetual canon, 225
Phrase, 17, 18, 35, 36, 37, 62, 94, 99, 101, 108, 137, 161
Pitch balance, 17, 19
Pitch location, 17, 81, 112, 132, 134, 194, 201, 209
Polyrhythms, 229
Polytonality, 230
Preparation, 48, 51

Quadruple counterpoint, 182
Quintuple counterpoint, 185

Range, 16, 171, 172
Resolution, 32, 44, 52, 58, 83, 89, 94, 147, 151
Rests, 138, 156, 158, 216

Retrograde, 104, 221
Rhythm, 26, 27, 35, 38, 105, 192, 229
Rhythmic activity, 78, 95
Rhythmic pattern, 74, 105, 122, 229
Riddle canon, 225
Root progression, 41, 114

Scarlatti, A., 164
Scarlatti, D., 93
Schubert, 21, 31, 32, 55, 64, 102
Schumann, 18, 28, 32, 52, 65, 108, 132, 155, 212
Secondary dominants, 43, 186, 195
Sequence, 113, 126, 174, 181, 183
Seventh chord, 126, 143
Similar motion, 83, 86, 89, 125, 146, 156
Six-four chord, 91, 127
Six-part counterpoint, 161
Spacing, 132, 150, 158
Static harmony, 69, 192, 195
Stretto, 190
Strong beat, 30, 38, 39, 70
Subdominant seventh chord, 45
Submediant seventh chord, 51, 127
Suspension, 45, 50, 58, 59, 63, 91, 126, 180
Symbols, 41, 127
Syncopation, 54, 65, 78, 83, 193

Tchaikowsky, 47

Tendency tones, 44, 89, 95, 126
Texture, 132, 143, 151, 156, 158, 161, 188, 195, 210, 211, 216, 228, 230
Thirteenth chord, 45, 52, 152
Three-part canon, 208, 220
Three-part counterpoint, 118
Time interval, 190, 199, 206, 208, 212
Tonal degrees, 94, 95, 195, 201, 213
Tonality, 41, 94, 126, 145, 176, 198, 202, 212
Tonic ninth chord, 52
Transposition, 103, 107, 167, 195, 199
Triple counterpoint, 180
Tritone, 94, 125, 176
Twelve-tone system, 230
Twentieth century, 228
Two-part canon, 188
Two-part counterpoint, 72

Unison, 81, 83, 136
Up-beat, 30, 39, 99, 100

Vertical sonority, 90, 129, 145, 152, 158, 229
Vivaldi, 105
Voice-leading, 90

Wagner, 43
Weak beat, 30, 39
Weber, 48

Books That Live

THE NORTON IMPRINT ON A BOOK
MEANS THAT IN THE PUBLISHER'S
ESTIMATION IT IS A BOOK NOT FOR A
SINGLE SEASON BUT FOR THE YEARS

W · W · NORTON & COMPANY · INC ·